The Dominican order and convocation : a study of the growth of representation in the church during the thirteenth century

Ernest Barker

B

THE DOMINICAN ORDER
AND CONVOCATION

A STUDY OF THE GROWTH OF REPRESENTATION

IN THE CHURCH

DURING THE THIRTEENTH CENTURY

BY

ERNEST BARKER, M.A.

FELLOW OF ST. JOHN'S COLLEGE
AND FORMERLY FELLOW OF MERTON COLLEGE, OXFORD

OXFORD
AT THE CLARENDON PRESS
1913

FEB 26 1953

OXFORD UNIVERSITY PRESS

LONDON   EDINBURGH   GLASGOW   NEW YORK
TORONTO   MELBOURNE   BOMBAY

HUMPHREY MILFORD M A.
PUBLISHER TO THE UNIVERSITY

PREFACE

THIS brief study would not have been written had it not been for M. Bémont, the Editor of the *Revue Historique*, and Honorary Doctor of Letters in the University of Oxford. He is unconscious of his influence: it is none the less real. He has done so much to illuminate the English history of the thirteenth century, that he must not be surprised if others try to use the light he has shed to explore new paths.

I owe a large debt of gratitude to my old pupil, Father Bede Jarrett, of the Order of Preachers. When we were once discussing together the development of representation, and I was urging the point I have urged here, that the Church supplied both the idea of representation and its rules of procedure, he suggested to me that the influence of his own Order must have been considerable within the Church, and he gave me my first knowledge of the organization of his Order. He has increased my debt of late by sending me some references which he had collected. I would refer any of my readers who may be interested in the Dominican Order to Father Jarrett's article in the *Home Counties Magazine* for June 1910 on 'Friar Confessors of English Kings', and to his pamphlet on the Dominicans published by the Catholic Truth Society.

Mr. A. G. Little has been good enough to read this study, and to save me from some errors into which I had fallen. The kindness of the author of the *Grey Friars in Oxford* is all the greater, as I have myself sought to exalt the Black Friars.

I should explain that this study was originally intended for a brief article. As I worked upon it, it outgrew the limits of my original intention, and ceasing to be a brief article almost grew into a small book. I have published it as it stands (though I would gladly have carried further some lines of inquiry which are here merely suggested), because other engagements prevent me from devoting myself to the subject for some time to come, and because I thought that such results as I had attained might possibly be of some immediate use to students of the history of institutions.

E. B.

OXFORD, *March*, 1913.

CONTENTS

PART I

THE DOMINICAN ORDER.

PART II

THE ENGLISH CONVOCATION.

INTRODUCTORY

THE Church of the thirteenth century shows a marked development, on its institutional side, of the principle and practice of representation Three great Councils of the Church are held: representatives appear in them all. The provincial synods cease to be composed of bishops and abbots only; representatives, first of cathedral clergy, and then— in England but in England only—of the diocesan clergy, enter. The great Orders of the Friars are penetrated by representation. It appears first in the Dominicans: it is copied from them by the Franciscans. In the same century representation begins to appear in the State. In Spain, indeed, it has already appeared in the last half of the twelfth century: in France it does not properly appear, except in local assemblies, until the beginning of the fourteenth. But in England, at any rate, the development of representation in the State synchronizes with the thirteenth century : a representative parliament begins to be seen in the middle of the century, and is fully grown by its end.

What was the history of the different phases of this movement, and what were their relations to one another? These are questions too large for their solution to be attempted here. Even if we confine ourselves to the Church, we have still a vast field of research. But an account of the organization of the Dominicans, who offer the most finished model of representative institutions, and a study of that development of the provincial synod in England which led to the inclusion of clerical proctors, may together serve to elucidate to some extent the institutional development which marks the thirteenth century. In the course of these inquiries we shall be led to look into the sources of the Dominican organization, and the extent of its influence (if any influence can be traced) on other contemporary developments of the same kind ; and we shall have to ask why the English synod developed on somewhat different lines from those of other countries, and how far the composition and procedure of that synod acted as a model or precedent for our national parliament.

PART I

THE DOMINICAN ORDER

HISTORY has not been unmindful of the friars ; and least of all, perhaps, in England have the friars of the thirteenth century gone unrecorded. Mr. Little has laboured on the records of the Franciscans with ungrudging love ; and the British Society of Franciscan Studies is itself an 'order' in their honour. But there were Black Friars as well as Grey Friars ; a St. Dominic as well as a St. Francis. English historians have not been equally kind to both.[1] It is true that St. Francis was indeed a saint, and St. Dominic rather a statesman Personality attracts the historian as much as the contemporary ; there are men living amongst us about whom we cannot but think and talk, and there are men who have lived amongst us about whom we cannot but think and write. The riches of the personality of *il poverello* were more abounding than those of the canon of Osma ; he who espoused Poverty, and sang the Canticle of the Sun, who bore on his body the wound-prints, and talked with the birds as a brother, was made of other stuff than the founder of the Order which administered the Inquisition.[2] Yet St. Dominic, like that other Spaniard who founded the Jesuit Order, was a constructive statesman ; and those who find in the study of institutions a charm as great as in the study of personalities are bound to look at his building, to discover its materials and to trace its influence. He had an eye for the needs of the occasion ; he could divine the proper methods for meeting

[1] Mr. Davis, for instance, in *England under the Normans and Angevins*, mentions the existence of the Dominicans, indeed, but devotes all his space to the Franciscans. Professor Tout (*The Political History of England*, 1216-1377) devotes more space to the Dominicans, and his sketch of their history in England (pp. 84-92) is very useful.

[2] On the real nature of the relation of the Dominicans to the Inquisition (they administered it reluctantly and often under compulsion) see Mandonnet in the *Catholic Encyclopaedia*, s v. Preachers, 368 B.

those needs with success. His followers said of him that
he always ' looked to the end' before he spoke ; 'and therefore seldom if ever did he consent to change a decision once
enunciated with due deliberation.'[3]   He had besides a con-
suming zeal for study, which alone could make a full 'preacher',
and for whose sake he commanded the student (exactly as
Plato commanded the guardian) to abandon all possessions or
hope of possessions which might distract the mind from its
work.[4]   The student of learning and its history must remember St. Dominic even before St. Francis.   After all, the
Franciscans are here, as they are in their organization, the
debtors and disciples of the Dominicans.   Study is original
and essential to the Dominicans, it is an afterthought with
the Franciscans ;[5] and the reorganization of the Franciscan
Order in the chapter general of 1239 is on Dominican lines.[6]
As for England—and it is with England that we are mainly
concerned—let us remind ourselves that the Dominicans had
been at work here for some three years before the Franciscans
arrived.   Gilbert of Freynet came to Oxford in the autumn of
1221, and when the Franciscans arrived at the end of 1224,
he gave them a cordial welcome until they could house
themselves.

[3] 'It has been said that it is St. Dominic's misfortune to be always
compared with St. Francis.   It seems to me that he need not be afraid of
this comparison.   St Dominic is *ein gereifter Charakter*, St Francis *eine
glucklıche Natur*'—Hauck, *Kirchengeschichte Deutschlands*, iv 387.
[4] *Instituerunt possessiones non habere, ne praedicatoris officium impe-
diretur sollicitudine terrenorum* ; Ehrle-Denifle, *Archiv fur Litteratur-
und Kirchengeschichte*, i. 182, n. 1.   Father Denifle maintains that
poverty is as original with the Dominicans as with the Franciscans
(cf. Hauck, *op. cit.*, iv. 387)   The object of the cult of poverty is different ;
St. Francis was poor for the sake of his own salvation, and that he might
imitate in his lowliness the example of his lowly Master ; St. Dominic
chose poverty that he might be the more free for study, and thereby for
preaching, and thereby for the salvation of others.   Professor Tout,
following the ordinary view, implies that Dominican poverty is the result
of imitation of the Franciscans : ' St. Dominic yielded to the fascination
of the Umbrian enthusiast, and inculcated on his Order a complete
renunciation of worldly goods' (*op. cit.*, p. 84).   It was in 1220 that the
Order adopted poverty.   From 1216 to 1220 it had enjoyed revenues, but
not possessions , in 1220 it gave up both (Mandonnet, *op cit.*)
[5] Ehrle-Denifle, *Archiv*, i. 184.
[6] Cf. Bohmer, *Analekten zur Geschichte des Franciscus von Assisi,*
Regesten, *s. a.* 1239, and Ehrle-Denifle, *Archiv*, vi. 20 sqq.

We have attributed to St. Dominic constructive statesmanship. What then was the organization which he constructed ;
what were the materials he used ; and how far was the
organization which he gave to his Order a model for other
builders? Briefly, we may say that St. Dominic founded an
Order belonging to the genus, not of 'religious', but of clerks ;
that these clerks belonged to the species of clerks called
canons regular ; and that the precise variety of canons regular
imitated by St. Dominic was the Praemonstratensian. The
Dominicans are clerks who form a body of regular canons,
after the model of Prémontié Their statutes are avowedly
modelled on those of the Praemonstratensians ;[7] and, like the
Praemonstratensians and other regular canons, the friars of the
Order have the cure of souls. But there is a great difference
between the Dominican and the Praemonstratensian. The
latter belongs to a particular abbey, and has cure of souls
in a particular parish. The Dominican is general and uni-
versal. He belongs to a house, to a province, but far more to
the whole Order ; and he has a cure of souls wherever he may
preach. He is delocalized, and he is centralized. He is
delocalized , he is not under the vow of *stabilitas*. He is not
a member of a particular abbey, in charge of a particular
parish that is under that abbey ; he is essentially a member
of the whole Order, who will preach at any point in the scope
of its action. He is centralized. He is not primarily under
the control of a particular abbey ; he is a soldier in a *militia
spiritualis* controlled by its generalissimo. His daily discipline, modelled though it may be on the Praemonstratensian,
is consequently different. . A member of an army of ubiquitous
preachers, he must not do the things that will hinder preaching, and he must do all the things that will foster preaching.
He need not be concerned unduly with fasting and the regular
hours of devotion ; for the sake of preaching and the study

---

[7] Ehrle-Denifle, *Archiv*, i. 172 sqq. Father Denifle quotes the words
of Humbert, the fifth master of the Order: 'The constitutions are largely
taken from those of the Praemonstratensians, who reformed the order of
regular canons, and excelled especially in the government of their order
by general chapters and visitations.'

which preaching needs he may have dispensation [8]   He need not labour with his hands: the Dominicans were the first Order to abandon manual work, and leave it to *conversi* ; and St. Dominic even proposed at Bologna, though the proposal was not adopted by the Chapter, that these lay brethren should be supreme in administration and temporal things, in order that the friars might be free for study and preaching. What a friar must do, must always and only do, is to study and to preach ; to study, that he may preach, and to preach from the fruits of his study.

Thus the old Praemonstratensian model slips away.   There was a strong element of local feeling in the model ; there was a devotion of the canon to the abbey, of daughter-abbey to mother-abbey, of all to Prémontré ; the Dominicans knew none of these things.   There was an aristocratic flavour in the organization of the model.   It was a decentralized aristocracy, except for the annual colloquy (always at Prémontré, and with obedience to the abbot thereof and his abbey), which however only consisted of abbots ; [9]   the Dominican government is otherwise.   There was, again, something of the old monastic habit in their discipline—something of labour and of regular hours : the Dominican discipline is different.   In the matter of organization especially St. Dominic must be held to be practically independent.   Two things he borrowed—the chapter general (but this is Cistercian in origin),[10] and the *annui circa-*

<hr/>

[8] Mandonnet makes a very interesting remark on this point. He points out that the Dominican Order contained two somewhat discrepant elements—the monastic-canonical element, inherited from the Praemonstratensian model, which made for the ascetic life and the *vita contemplativa*, and produced ascetics and mystics ; and the clerical-apostolic element, the essential new element, which made for the active life of study and preaching, and produced great doctors and apostles. There is a struggle between the two elements ; the former tends to check the latter   The practice of dispensation is meant to ease the struggle, and to secure a free field for study and preaching   But the rigid and ascetic element in the Order set its face against dispensation, and a certain dualism continued to mark the life of the Order

[9] Martène, *De antiquis ecclesiae ritibus*, iii. 334 (Distinction iv, § 1). Martène prints the original constitutions ; for their later form cf. *Statuta Praemonstrat.* (Paris, 1632), p 188.   In the later form the institution of *definitores*, which we shall find among the Dominicans, appears (p 194) ; but it is not in the early statutes.

[10] Cf. Viollet, *Histoire des Institutions de la France*, ii. 381.   The

tores, or visitors, two in number, elected annually by the abbots of a *circaria* or circle to visit the abbeys of the circle.[11] But the general lines of Dominican organization are independent of the Praemonstratensian, just as, and just because, the aims and objects of the Dominicans are different from those of the Praemonstratensians.

The main features of the organization of the Dominican Order were already fixed in the year 1221, by the labours of the two chapters which had sat at Bologna under the presidency of St. Dominic in 1220 and 1221.[12] It is a point of some importance for our inquiry that the organization of the Order should have been completed in the very chapter which made England a province and dispatched Gilbert of Freynet to England. Of the constitutions of 1221 we possess no copy, but we possess a copy of the redaction made at Paris in 1228. In that year we read that there were gathered at Paris, in the convent of St. James (from which the Dominicans at Paris were called Jacobins), round the Master-General Jordan, the priors of the provinces, each with two *definitores* deputed by the provincial chapters, to whom all the friars had transferred their votes (*vota sua*), giving them plenary authority to act. This assembly added a number of constitutions (as, for instance, against the holding of property; concerning the removal of appeals, against the making of constitutions unless approved by three successive chapters general—a provision which reminds us of the Parliament Act

Cistercians early established provincial chapters also, and they are prescribed as a rule for the other monks who have not hitherto held such chapters in the twelfth canon of the Fourth Lateran Council (*infra*, 11, n. 12)

[11] See note 7. The *circatores* had to be abbots of abbeys in the *circaria*: Martène, p 335, Dist. iv, § 7. In the Dominican Order the visitors are friars freely elected In the later constitutions of the Praemonstratensians provision is made for regular chapters in the *circariae*, attended not only by abbots and priors, but by one representative pastor from each abbey, to be deputed by the other pastors (*op. cit.*, p. 206). But this seems, like the instance quoted in note 9, to be imitation by the Praemonstratensians of the Dominican model in later days.

[12] It was in 1216 that St. Dominic had adopted the 'rule' of St. Augustine, which regulated the life of canons regular, and had added *consuetudines* of his own for the guidance of the Order But the *constitutiones* of 1220 are the 'essential and original basis of Dominican legislation' (Mandonnet, in the *Catholic Encyclopaedia*, s. v. Preachers).

of 1911—and against riding, or the eating of flesh except in illness) ;[13] and these constitutions, along with the original statutes of 1220 and 1221, foim the redaction of 1228.[14] The importance of the assembly of 1228 lies not only in its work, but in its own composition. Already we see representative institutions at work, and we aie justified in believing that those institutions were incorporated into the Oider in the chapters of 1220 and 1221, and were part of the working constitution when it came to England in 1221.[15]

In 1221 the Order was divided into eight provinces (analogous to the Praemonstratensian *circariae*, but still more to the *pays* of the Hospitallers), each containing a number of houses (*conventus*). The Order was to be governed by a master-general; the province by a provincial prior; the convent, which must contain at least twelve friars, by a conventual prior. We have to considei the method of the election of these officers, and the extent to which their action is accompanied or controlled by iepresentative bodies. (1) The conventual prior is elected by the friars of his convent (Dist. ii, § 24),[16] the provincial prior is elected by a provincial chapter composed of the conventual priors of the province and two friars from each convent elected by a full meeting of all the friars of the convent (Dist. ii, § 15),[17] the master-general is elected by a general chapter composed of the piovincial priors

[13] For the assembly of 1228 see *Constitutiones Fratrum S. Ordinis Praedicatorum*, Paris, 1886, pp. 478-9. I owe my copy of this book to the generosity of my old pupil, the Rev. Bede Jarrett, O P.

[14] The redaction of 1228 is printed by Father Denifle in Ehrle-Denifle, *Archiv*, i, p. 196 sqq., with an introduction which I have used freely Father Denifle also prints a reconstruction of the redaction of 1239-41 (made by Raymond of Pennaforte, third Master of the Order), *Archiv*, v. 530 sqq   The last redaction in the thirteenth century is that of Humbert, the fifth Master, in 1256.

[15] Theodoric of Apoldia tells us, as a matter of fact, that St. Dominic decided in 1220 at Bologna that *definitores* should be appointed, with power over himself as master and over the whole chapter, to define, decree, and ordain all things as long as the chapter should last   'Decrevit ut statuerentur definitores, qui haberent potestatem super ipsum et totum capitulum diffiniendi statuendi ordinandi, donec duraret capitulum' (*Acta Sanct.*, August, i 594)

[16] The references are all, unless otherwise stated, to the Constitutions of 1228 as printed in Ehrle-Denifle, *Archiv*, i, pp. 196 sqq.

[17] This is slightly altered in the modern constitutions ; see *op cit*, P 337

and two friars from each province elected by the provincial chapter (Dist. ii, § 10) [18] The free use of election, and of representatives in election, clearly emerges. (2) By the side of the elected officials stand assemblies also in part elected. Of the *capitulum quotidianum* in each convent we need not speak; but the constitution and action of the provincial chapter and the chapter general are vital to our argument. The provincial chapter consists of the priors of the convents of the province, of the general preachers of the province (friars, that is to say, who have studied theology for three years, Dist ii, § 31), and of a representative elected by each convent (Dist. ii, § 1). For its guidance the provincial chapter annually elects a committee of four *definitores* from the more discreet and proper friars.[19] It is the office of this committee to treat and define all things with the provincial prior, it has the power of hearing and amending excesses of the provincial prior, whom it may, in case of need, suspend (Dist ii, § 2–3). The chapter general is constituted in the same manner.[20] There is a general body and there is an effective inner circle of *definitores*. The general body consists of conventual priors with their *socii* and the general preachers of the province in which the general chapter is being held (Dist ii, § 12) The arrangement for the constitution of the inner circle of *definitores* is peculiar (Dist. ii, §§ 5–8) According to the constitutions of 1228 the general chapters are held annually. In two successive annual chapters the *definitores* are recruited by election: one is elected for each province by the provincial chapter, and each has a *socius* assigned to him by the provincial prior and *definitores* to take his place if he cannot be present at the general chapter. In every third general chapter the *definitores* cease to be an elected body: the provincial priors ex officio and by themselves

---

[18] Four provinces created since 1221 are to send each its provincial prior and *one* friar to the chapter.

[19] The institution of *definitores* (' qui jouent à peu près le rôle des commissaires dans nos assemblées délibérantes ', Viollet, *op. cit.*, ii 382) becomes common in the thirteenth century, and appears for instance in the constitution of the Cluniac Order.

[20] The chapters general met alternately at Paris and Bologna till 1244. Afterwards they met in different places (e. g. London in 1250), and thus knowledge of the organization of the Order would be spread.

act as *definitores* for the year. Any new constitution must pass through three successive chapters general before it is finally valid. In this way the provincial priors get some share of authority, while the greater weight is nevertheless reserved for the elective *definitores*.[21] The committee of *definitores*, whether elected or ex officio, is the chief organ. It defines, constitutes and treats all things; its members have plenary power, extending even to removal from office, over the master-general; and careful provision is made for counting a majority of their votes. Beyond the chapter general stands the *capitulum generalissimum*, a body which only met twice in the history of the Order—once in 1228, and once in 1236. It contains in one body, and in a single meeting, both provincial priors and elected *definitores*, *two* from each province, appointed by the provincial chapter. It was therefore equivalent to three successive chapters general of the ordinary kind; and consequently it could pass finally and at once, if there were urgent need, a new constitution.[22] Two further points may conclude this sketch of Dominican organization. St. Dominic borrowed from his Praemonstratensian model the office of *visitatores*, of whom four were to be elected from the friars of each province, assembled in their provincial chapter, to visit the province and to hear and amend all excesses (Dist. ii, § 19); but the fact that the visitors are to be elected from the friars, and not from the priors, is a democratic modification of the Praemonstratensian rule, which only allowed abbots to be elected as *circatores*. Further, he assigned to the provincial prior the same power and the same reverence in his province

[21] Humbert de Romanis (quoted in *Archiv*, vi 22–3) explains that among Orders like the Cistercian and Praemonstratensian the authority rests with the greater prelates, and they alone act as *definitores*; with the Franciscans authority is shared among the prelates and a number of their subjects; but among the Dominicans there is *abundantia discretionis etiam in subditis . . et ideo fiunt diffinitores apud nos non solum praelati majores, ut provinciales, sed etiam subditi quicunque per electionem in majore numero* Evidently he regards the Dominicans as carrying furthest what we should call the principle of democracy, and he is quite conscious of the strength of representation in his Order.

[22] See *Constitutiones S. Ord. Praedic.* (Paris, 1886), p. 478. The *capitulum generalissimum* is not mentioned in the constitutions of 1228, though they were passed in such a chapter; it is from the later constitutions that we learn its composition.

as that of the master-general, and he laid it down that on the death of the general master, the provincial priors should exercise the full powers of a general master (Dist. ii, § 16, § 9).

What are the general characteristics of this organization? In the first place it is democratic.   If Cluny is 'monarchical', if Cîteaux (and we may add Prémontié, in many respects modelled on Cîteaux) is 'aristocratical', we may call the friars democratic.[23]   There is no speech in their organization of abbots or of paternal authority coming from above; authority springs from the general body, and the officials are rather servants of that body than its lords. This democratic flavour is, as we shall see, almost as striking in the Franciscan as in the Dominican Order; but the whole mechanism of the latter Order, as it has been just described, is obviously democratic in comparison with previous Orders. True, the democracy is *de facto*, and in its actual working compatible and connected with what we may call Caesarism; the Master-General of the Order is often its moving spirit. But the point remains, that the constitutional arrangements, as they stand *de jure*, are of a kind which we should to-day call democratic.[24]   And, in the second place, it is a repre-

---

[23] H. O. Taylor, *The Mediaeval Mind*, i. 361–3. Mandonnet speaks of modern absolutist governments as showing 'little sympathy for the *democratic* constitution of the Preachers' (s. v. Preachers, 368 E, col 2).

[24] The Constitution of the Third Order (or Tertiaries) has not been described in the text; it is dubious whether the Third Order was instituted by St Dominic himself (see J Guiraud, *Life of St. Dominic*, English translation, p. 166), and the *Constitutiones S. Ord. Praed.* only give a transcription made from the papal registers in 1439, at the command of Eugenius IV, of a papal bull of Innocent VII which sets forth and confirms the rule of the brethren and sisters of the Third Order as hitherto observed (pp. 682–93). According to Mandonnet, the Rule of the Third Order dates from 1285, and was confirmed in 1286 by Honorius IV   Each Fraternity of Tertiaries, it appears, has its Master or Director, a friar appointed by the Master-General or Provincial Prior at the request of the Fraternity, and its Prior, an officer appointed by the Master with the counsel of the ancient of the Fraternity. Each year the Master and the ancients scrutinize the Prior and his actions. The Order of Tertiaries would spread knowledge of Dominican organization, and has in itself some approach to self-government.   But we must note (1) that the Rule of the Third Order of the Dominicans was modelled on that of the Franciscan brothers of Penance , and (2) that it was opposed by the Franciscans as an encroachment, and by some of the Dominicans as an excrescence, and it grew but slowly (Mandonnet, p. 369, col. 2).

sentative democracy.   There is repeatedly election of free representatives, who are not delegates, but have (as we read of the assembly of 1228) ‘plenary power, so that whatever is done by them shall remain firm and stable’.   The characteristic feature of the Order, says Mandonnet, is its elective system ; it is the general chapters, built largely on this system, which wield supreme power, and are the great regulators of Dominican life in the Middle Ages , from them springs that spirit of firmness and decision which marks the whole Order   Thirdly and lastly, the constitutions of the Order are clear-cut in their outline, and show something of a legal nicety and precision. ‘ It is the most perfect example that the Middle Ages have produced of the faculty of monastic corporations for constitution-building.’ [25]   Its institutions are adjusted to probable emergencies ; they define, for instance, the conditions of a valid majority ; they are institutions meant, and likely, to work.   We may conjecture that they will also be likely to impress men who come into contact with them,[26] and that they will tend to be imitated.   And if they are imitated, the use of representation is the thing which will in particular be imitated.

But before we can verify that conjecture, we must ask to what extent these institutions are original and to what extent they are unique.   Was St. Dominic borrowing ?   Did other orders or bodies share these institutions ?   We may lay it down at once that St. Dominic was not borrowing from the Franciscans ; but that is a point to which we shall have to return.   On the other hand, we may readily guess that the Military Orders contributed to his scheme of organization. They too formed a *militia spiritualis* ; they too followed, like the Dominicans, the rule of life of canons regular.

We shall perhaps do best, in seeking to trace the relations of the Dominican Order to the Military Orders, to consider the Hospitallers first.   Their connexion with Spain, and with

[25] Hauck, *Kirchengeschichte Deutschlands*, iv. 390.
[26] The Order spread widely, and would be well known in most countries   By 1228 there were eight provinces; by 1256 there were 5,000 priests in the Order (besides 2,000 other clergy and lay brethren) ; by 1277 there were 404 convents (Mandonnet)

St. Dominic's quarter of Spain, was early and intimate.   As early as 1116 they had received donations in Castile and Leon,[27] and when a grand master arose for Spain about 1170 (*magnus magister in V regnis Hispaniae*), he was specially accredited in Castile, which was under his immediate supervision.   About 1190, however, a separate organization was given to the Hospitallers of Castile and Leon, such as those of the other kingdoms had enjoyed before.   A priory of Castile and Leon is created : the chapter of the priory meets in 1190.[28] Its organization is likely to come to the notice of the young Dominic, who is studying in Palencia in 1190, and becomes a canon of Osma in 1194

The general basis of the organization of the Hospitallers is the sovereignty of the Chapter.   The general chapter of the whole Order is sovereign in legislation and discipline, but while reserving a right of control it leaves executive power to the Grand Master and the officers of his appointing, who are its delegates or representatives   The same principle applies to the subordinate chapters in their degree; it is the principle, in a sense, of representative or parliamentary government. At the centre the general chapter proper, in the twelfth and even in the thirteenth century, meets irregularly and at variable intervals.   Nor is it very determinate in its composition; the Grand Master summons the officials of the Holy Land, the priors of the West, and those of the simple knights whose discretion or testimony in any affair renders their presence necessary.   The regular and permanent body which the Grand Master consults (when it is not a matter of general legislation or discipline) is the ' Convent ', which is always in attendance and consists of the officers of the central administration.   If we see in this central government a germ of Dominican organization, we must admit that that organization is more highly differentiated and more strictly regular than its germ.   Locally, the Hospitallers are organized in commanderies or houses of brothers, living in community under a *praeceptor* or commander, and meeting every Sunday

---

[27] Delaville Le Roulx, *Les Hospitaliers*, p 377.
[28] Ibid., p 380.

in ordinary chapter; in priories, or groups of commanderies, under a prior, who holds a chapter of the priory about St. John's Day; and in grand commanderies, or groups of priories, under a grand commander.[29]   The chapter of the priory is open in theory to all the brethren of a priory ; in fact it is composed of the brethren resident at the chief place of the priory and of the commanders of commanderies attending as representatives of their knights.   There are here no representatives proper, as in the Dominican Order, and yet the spirit of this Military Order is, as we said above, in a sense representative.   The Chapter General is the one legislative authority. if it leaves administration to the officers, it nominates and controls those officers.   Each chapter, from the chapter general to the ordinary chapter, assists its superior in government, and shares with its superior in responsibility. The central officers must be renewed in each chapter general : they bear a burden rather than an honour (*onus non honos*) : they are servants of the chapter.[30]

The organization of the Templars was somewhat similar in detail, but somewhat different in spirit.   By the time that the organization of the Order was fixed (in the twenty-four years between Alexander III's bull *Omne datum optimum* of 1163 and the loss of Jerusalem in 1187) the Grand Master has achieved a great position.   He has indeed to consult the chapter general on all important matters, and to submit to its decision such matters as the alteration or repeal of a decision of a chapter, the alienation of property, and the military policy of the Order   But he has his own treasure, he has no *Conventus* at his side, but only two adjutants; and if he needs the consent of the chapter in appointing the Grand Praeceptors of provinces,[31] he appoints himself the lower

---

[29] The Grand Commandery is a *pays* or (in later phrase) a *langue* This suggests the Dominican provinces.   The nomenclature of the Hospitallers (e. g. *magister*) also suggests that of the Dominicans.

[30] In practice, as time went on, the Grand Master grew more autocratic, and in 1295 the knights ask for a permanent council of seven *definitores* at his side.

[31] Aragon and Portugal were provinces, but not Castile, though the Order had a position in Castile   Prutz, *Entwickelung und Untergang des Tempelherrenordens*, pp. 44, 61.

officers. Nor was there any great amount of local independence; the provincial praeceptors controlled the lower officers, who had little independence.[32]   It is to the Hospitallers rather than to the Templars that we must look for light on the Dominican Order; and we must admit that even if St. Dominic borrowed elements from the Hospitallers, he did not simply copy, and that he did not find there any use of representation.

We have considered the relations of St. Dominic to the Military Orders; but what of his relations to St. Francis? We are only concerned with those relations at one point; our one inquiry concerns the relations of Dominican to Franciscan organization. The earliest copy of the Franciscan Rule which we possess, the *regula non bullata*, whose date may be fixed as a little posterior to the end of May, 1221, enables us to give an answer.[33]   The rule is simple; it shows nothing of St Dominic's genius for organization. We hear of officials, 'ministers and servants of the other friars,' whose duty it is to visit and spiritually warn and comfort in all provinces and in places, and to give to friars their licence to preach   In each year each minister may assemble with his friars, wherever they will, to treat of the things that belong to God.   Every year the Italian *ministri* (the *ministri* outside Italy need only come once in three years) shall gather at Whitsuntide at the Church of St. Mary de Portiuncula, unless by the minister and servant of the whole Order it be otherwise ordained. The friars are now too numerous to permit of the old broad primary assemblies of all the 'brethren'. the last of those assemblies, held in 1221, had contained 5,000 members; and the old democratic gathering has now to give place to a *concilium principum*. In all this we have adumbrated the outlines of an organization; but St. Francis is not in love with organization   He will not have any one called prior,[34] but rather

---

[32] Prutz, *op. cit.*, pp. 42-4.

[33] The rule is printed in Bohmer, *Analekten zur Geschichte des Franciscus von Assisi*, pp. 7 sqq. We have no copy of the original rule of 1209 (The view has, however, been held that the *regula non bullata* is itself the original rule of 1209.)

[34] Is this possibly a reference to the Dominican title ? If so, St. Francis may have had the Dominican constitutions before him.

all called *fratres minores* ; he will not have the brethren bear
power or dominion, especially among themselves.   A friar is
not bound to obey a *minister* who commands anything against
the ' life' ; and the friars are to consider the doings of *ministri*
and *servi*, and if they are doing wrong after the third admoni-
tion, to renounce them in the Whitsuntide chapter.   Some of
these rules would be the despair of any statesman ; and some
of them (as for instance the rule authorizing a friar in disobeying
a *minister*) are dropped in the next redaction of the Rule we
possess—that of 1223 [35]   In this new redaction we also see an
advance in organization.   The titles *minister generalis* and
minister provincialis appear ; the general minister is to be
elected in a chapter general composed of provincial *ministri*
and *custodes*, the latter a new title, which designates the head
of a group of friars.   If the chapter, forming the *universitas* of
ministers and *custodes*, considers the general minister inade-
quate, it may elect another friar for custodian (*custos*) of the
Order.   After the general chapter the ministers and guardians
may severally, if they will, summon the friars in their ' custo-
dies' once to a chapter.   But the general chapter is now only
triennial , and the subsidiary chapters, which are to follow on
the general chapter, are therefore also intermittent.   It is not
chapters, but the general minister, of whom St. Francis thinks.
In his *Testamentum*, about 1226, he speaks of his obedience
to the general minister and the other guardians whom he is
pleased to give; 'and I wish so to be caught in his hands as
not to be able to go or to do outside my obedience and his
will'.[36]   If in the Dominican Order it is the General Master
and the Chapter who together form the sovereign body, it is
the General Minister, and the General Minister only, who is
sovereign in the Franciscan Order down to the revolution of
1239-40.   He is undisputed Caesar . he nominates subordinate
officers, and he legislates either without any chapter (Elias held
no chapters in his nine years' tenure of office from 1230 to 1239),

[35] A redaction of the year 1222 is lost (Bohmer, *op. cit.*, Introduction).
The redaction of 1223 is printed by Bohmer, pp 30 sqq.   For an account
of it, and of the constitutional history of the Franciscan Order in the
thirteenth century, see Ehrle in *Archiv fur Lit- und Kircheng.*, vi.
[36] See §§ 9-10 of the *Testamentum* in Bohmer.

or with a chapter composed only and entirely of officers whom he has himself appointed. There is a complete absence of representative institutions : the change introduced by Gregory IX in 1230, according to which the *custodes* of a province ceased to attend chapters in person, and elected one of their number to go in their stead, can hardly be called a step towards representation

Such was the organization of the Franciscan Order when it reached England in 1224. By 1240 that organization had been greatly changed ; but it had been changed by being assimilated to the Dominican model. Each of the three main features of the revolution achieved in the two chapters of 1239 and 1240 is a Dominican feature. The powers of the general minister and his subordinates are restricted, and partially, in some cases wholly, transferred to the general and provincial chapters. The nomination of subordinate officers passes out of the hands of the general minister ; they are henceforth appointed by the free choice, or at any rate with the consent, of the chapters. Finally, provision was made, exactly on the Dominican model,[37] for the election of *definitores* to attend the general chapter ; and henceforth a freely elected representative element was added to the officials who had hitherto alone composed the chapter. This was the form of organization definitely codified at Narbonne in 1260, and henceforth regular.[38] It follows, therefore, that if we are looking for the

[37] Strictly speaking, the exact Dominican model was only followed once, or perhaps twice ; cf *Eccleston* (ed. A G. Little), p 87, and n. ᵃ ; cf also Ehrle, *Archiv*, vi. 20 sqq. The Franciscan chapter general, by 1260, differs from the Dominican in being triennial, not annual ; and in admitting the provincial minister in every chapter to the committee of *definitores*

[38] See Ehrle, *Archiv*, vi, who prints the Constitutions of 1260 In these constitutions we may note (1) the *guardiani* and *custodes* are nominated by the provincial minister with counsel and consent (pp. 127–8), the provincial minister is elected by the provincial chapter (p. 125), and the general minister is elected by the provincial ministers and *custodes* (p. 123); (2) the annual provincial chapter consists of *custodes* and *fratres* of the province, but to avoid a multitude of members there is an election in each convent of one *discretus* (p 129) : four *definitores* are selected by three men named by the minister, the *custos*, and the guardian of the place of the chapter (p 131) , (3) the triennial general chapter is attended by the provincial ministers each with a *socius*, by one *custos* from each province elected by the *custodes* (as laid down in 1230), and by one *discretus*

organization of the friars, and the effect of that organization on the rest of the Church, we must start from the Dominican Order. The early Franciscan organization is too simple and inchoate to have served as a model: the later Franciscan organization is itself based on the Dominican. But we may allow, nevertheless, that part of the early Franciscan organization (the broad primary assembly down to 1221, and the whole tone of the *regula non bullata*) showed a still stronger democratic tendency than that of the Dominicans, and would foster a feeling for liberty such as inspires the Franciscan author of the Song of Lewes; and we may allow that the Dominican organization acted through the Franciscans, who had modelled themselves upon it, as well as through the Dominicans themselves.[39] Indeed we may go further, and admit that the type of institutions employed by the Dominicans was becoming common among religious orders generally in the thirteenth century.[40] There was a movement towards centralization; and this movement involved on the one hand a central executive, on the other hand a central legislature, while the central legislature needed the guidance of a committee like the Dominican *definitores*, and the central executive needed the help of local representatives like the Praemonstratensian *circatores* and Dominican visitors. To this movement the Military Orders had contributed, ruled as they were by grand masters and general chapters; to it the widespread Cistercians had contributed, united as they were by the annual chapters at Cîteaux in a fraternal bond of charity; to it the Praemonstratensians had contributed, divided as they were into circles, from which possibly the provinces of the Military Orders, and thus indirectly those of the Friars, were borrowed. Of this movement the organization of the Friars is the culmination, though even old Orders like Cluny came under its

elected by the provincial chapter—the *ministri* and *discreti* acting as *definitores* (p. 134)

[39] M Viollet inverts the truth when he says: *La constitution des Dominicains, je dirais volontiers politique, fut calquée sur la constitution franciscaine (op. cit, ii. 392)*

[40] See Viollet, *op. cit*, ii. 381. Thus even the Benedictines were enjoined by a canon of the fourth Lateran Council to hold provincial chapters, in which *visitatores* were to be elected; cf. *infra*, ii. n. 12.

influence.[41]   Nevertheless we would still urge that the precise form which the culmination took is due to the statesmanship of St. Dominic; and we would further urge that the Dominican Order is original and unique in its use of representatives elected by local communities for the conduct of the affairs of the Order.

It was this use of representatives elected by local communities which was perhaps imitated in England by the secular clergy, and which gave us our representative Convocation. For whatever the disputes and struggles between the Orders and the secular clergy, it cannot be denied that the Orders represented the advance guard of the Church militant, and that they drew after them the seculars to a higher level of discipline and a more developed form of organization.   The Orders were the field for progressive experimentation· they represented, particularly in the field of organization, the liberal and radical element of the Church.   Each new Order, however much it might lean on the past and on previous models, meant a new possibility of institutional development.   The Dominicans had availed themselves of that possibility; and the vogue and the prestige which this compact and admirably organized community enjoyed in the thirteenth century, both with statesmen like de Montfort and prelates like Langton, would tend to the spread of its institutions.   Here was an approved type; and it is a law of human nature that the approved type should at once be imitated.   The majority of the religious Orders of the thirteenth century, says Mandonnet, followed quite closely Dominican legislation, and the Church considered it the typical rule for new foundations.[42]

How far, if at all, secular models were followed by St Dominic in his adoption of this principle of the election of representatives by local communities it is difficult to say.

[41] In the course of the thirteenth century Cluny acquired a chapter general, with *definitores* elected by the chapter general (not, be it noted, by local units, as in the Dominican Order)   See *supra*, n. 19

[42] The Friars of the Sack adopted the Dominican organization *in toto*: cf *E. H R.*, ix. 121 sqq.   Grosseteste, in his struggle with his chapter, appeals to the example of Dominican practice in the matter of visitations (*Epistolae*, pp 377–8).

One naturally turns to Spain and to Southern France. The early constitutional history of Spain has still to be written. The first meeting of the Castilian Cortes at which representatives of towns weie present was in 1169.[43] In Leon itself, St. Dominic's home, we hear of *electi cives* (*deputados ó procuradores de las ciudades*) attending along with all the bishops and magnates at a meeting in 1188, and again in 1208.[44] These things were doubtless known to St. Dominic (who in 1188 was canon of Osma in Leon). How far they influenced him—how far the founder of an ecclesiastical Order would take heed of any but ecclesiastical precedents—we cannot say If we could tell at what date prelates and chapters of cathedral and collegiate churches began to send plenipotentiary representatives to the Cortes, as we are told they did,[45] we might be able to make some tentative statement; but in default of more precise knowledge we can only return an *ignoramus*. We do not know whether Spanish precedent influenced St Dominic all that we know is that communities (*universidades* and especially *ciudades*) were represented in Spain, and that, at any rate in time, these representatives weie of the nature of proctors, and had powers of attorney.

Southern France, the home of Roman influence and of

[43] Stubbs, *Const. Hist.* ii 168, Schafer, *Spanien*, iv. 192 The meeting was at Burgos. In Aragon *procuradores* of towns and districts are attested at Huesca in 1162: Schafer, iii 208. In Aragon the *cortes* were more settled and permanent in form than in Castile (ibid, p 229, n) Here there appeared *promovedores*, who are like the ecclesiastical *definitores*, and whose office it was to submit matters to the proper 'arm' (*brazo*, or House), to receive its decision, and to get that decision written down by a notary (ibid, p 232). We may notice (ibid., p 216) that the fourth arm in Aragon is the *brazo de universidades*, or house of corporations or communities (cf. our House of Commons, or *domus communitatum*). According to one historian of Spain (Burke, i. 343) every corporation was entitled in theory to send a representative. Further, the representatives of these bodies are *personeros*, or *procuradores*: they have powers of attorney, sometimes in writing. Here we have the two cardinal ideas of the English parliament under Edward I,—the representation of communities, and the procuratorial character of such representation (cf. the Writ of Summons of the parliament of 1295). But these ideas are later than the twelfth century, though in the absence of any readily accessible 'constitutional documents' for Spanish history it is difficult to fix the date of their emergence

[44] *Colección de Cortes*, Madrid, 1885.

[45] Schafer, *op. cit.*, iv. 221. The first instance I have noted of proctors of chapters in Spanish provincial synods is in 1302 (*infra*, ii. n. 37).

a precocious culture, gives us cases of representation early in
the thirteenth century.   In Languedoc, at the end of the
twelfth century, we find two towns repiesented at the *curia
generalis* of their lord   In 1212 Simon de Montfort summons
to a great parliament at Pamiers bishops, nobles, and notable
burgesses, and has statutes made therein for the regulation of
the country ; and a similar assembly was held at Béziers after
his son Amaury had ceded Languedoc to Louis VIII.[46]   The
representatives at another assembly at Béziers (but this is not
until 1271) bring procuratoiial powers from their towns.   The
interest of these instances lies in the fact that St. Dominic was
closely connected, after about 1203, with the South of France,
and with the elder Simon de Montfort.   When one sees
St. Dominic and de Montfort in conjunction in Southern
France—when one remembers what St. Dominic did for the
principle of representation in the Church, and de Montfort's
son for that piinciple in the State—one is tempted to find some
common ground for their allegiance to the piinciple, and to
find that common ground in Southern France   But that would
be pure conjecture ; and it would be safer to say that the common ground between the two was a common adhesion to the
same idea, an idea always cherished by the Church, of power
as a tiust given by the community, and of the community as
in some sense sovereign of itself, even if it delegates its sovereignty to a *magister*.   It is an idea with a long history.   It
is expressed by Ulpian (*Quod principi placuit legis habet vigo-
rem, utpote cum populus . . . ei et in eum omne suum imperium
et potestatem conferat*) : it is expressed in Peter Damiani
(*Potestas est in populo A summo data Domino*) : it is expressed
in the Song of Lewes by de Montfort's partisan   It undeilies
the organization of the Hospitallers . it underlies that of the
Dominicans.   Whenever men conceive of a group clearly and
strongly as a community or brotherhood, they must conceive
of it as sovereign of itself ; whenever they seek to realize that
self-sovereignty in deed as well as in word, they are driven
beyond the conception of power as in its nature representative
to the actual use of iepresentative institutions.   The Military

[46] Viollet, *Histoire des institutions de la France*, iii pp. 180-1

Orders and the Friars were such a brotherhood (*commilitones* and *fratres*), and in the friars, if not in the knights, the full consequences of their brotherhood were drawn. Perhaps through St. Dominic, perhaps through the example of Southern France, perhaps independently, the family of de Montfort (or so to some of us it may seem) became imbued with this conception—a conception continued by the Lancastrians, their dispossessors and successors (if sometimes, as with Thomas of Lancaster, for selfish ends, and sometimes, as with Henry IV, under compulsion), and continued further in the Whig theory of Locke.

Let us for a moment seek to realize the vogue of the Dominicans in England during the thirteenth century, before we seek to trace the development of representation in the provincial synods of the Church. Even before the Dominican mission came to England in 1221, connexions had been knit between the Order and England   St. Dominic was already the close friend of the elder Simon de Montfort ; Laurence of England was already a friar.[47]   When Gilbert of Freynet came in 1221, he travelled with his twelve brethren in the company of Peter des Roches, Bishop of Winchester, who was returning from the Holy Land by way of Bologna   When he reached Canterbury, he was cordially received by the great Langton (father of Magna Carta, and father of a representative Convocation), at whose request he preached in a church where Langton himself should have preached. The archbishop was so greatly edified by his discourse, that ever afterwards he bore a special affection for the Dominicans [48]   At the end of the year Gilbert settled in Oxford, and St. Edward's School was soon begun. A house was established in London at Holborn ; de Montfort founded another in Leicester ; and the Order was multiplied. In 1229, after a great dispute of town and gown at Paris,[49] there was an emigration of Dominicans to Oxford ; and the Master himself, Jordan, came to Oxford, where Grosseteste met him, and was admitted by his 'sweet

[47] J. Guiraud, *Life of St. Dominic* (Eng. trans.), p. 105.

[48] Trivet, *Annales*, s.a 1221 *toto suo tempore religionem fratrum Praedicatorum et officium prosecutus est gratia et favore.*

[49] Rashdall, *History of Mediaeval Universities*, 1 337.

affability' to many conversations.   In the house at Oxford
was held the Mad Parliament in 1258, and a general chapter
of the Order in 1280; in the house at Holborn general
chapters assembled in 1250 and 1263, and at the latter
St. Thomas Aquinas was present as *definitor* of the Roman
province.   Grosseteste, friendly as he was with the Franciscans,
was also the friend of the Dominicans.   As soon as he
becomes bishop of Lincoln, in 1235, he writes to the
provincial prior, and afterwards to the provincial prior and
the *definitores* sitting in provincial chapter at York, to ask
for the attendance of two friars, John of St. Giles and another,
for the ensuing year.   He seems to have had two Dominican
friars in regular attendance: in 1242 he complains to the
provincial prior that they are frequently changed   What he
did himself he would have had Canterbury do. in 1245 he
writes to a cardinal to urge that the archbishop should be supported on either hand by friars from the two Orders, who
alone can give such support as he needs [50]   The archbishop
who succeeded Boniface was himself a Dominican , Kilwardby,
Archbishop of Canterbury from 1273 to 1278, had been Provincial Prior.   Eleanor of Castile, the wife of Edward I, was
greatly attached to the Order, and contemplated the founda-
tion of a convent of Sisters, which was eventually founded by
her grandson Edward III.   From all this it is plain that the
Dominicans and their institutions were well known in the
central places of England, at Oxford and at London ; we can see
that the heads of Church and of State, Langton and Kilwardby,
de Montfort and Edward I, were familiar with the Order.

Meanwhile much was done by English Dominicans in the
realm of learning.[51] We read of nearly a dozen writers and
commentators in this century.   Kilwardby, representing the

---

[50] Grosseteste, *Epistolae*, pp. 59 61, 305, 336   Trivet, *Annales*, s.a. 1253
[51] See Ehrle-Denifle, *Archiv*, ii. 227 sqq.; Bémont, *Simon de Montfort*,
p. 85, and Mandonnet, 363 sqq. Dominican studies were arranged
on the following plan   In each convent there was a doctor, who gave
lectures which all the friars, even the prior, must attend, and which secular
clerks could attend · larger convents were termed *studia sollennia*.   The
studium generale in a University was conducted by a master or regent,
and two bachelors, one a *biblicus*, who lectured for a year on the Bible, the
other a *sententiarius*, who lectured for two years on the Sentences.   The
work done by the Dominicans on biblical concordances and on the

old Augustinian and pre-Thomist tradition, wrote on Aristotle's
Organon (including the Prior and Posterior Analytics), on
Aristotle's physical and metaphysical writings (including the
De Anima); on Priscian, on the Sentences of Peter the
Lombard, on the unity of forms, on the origin and division
of knowledge, and on the nature of relation [52]   William, afterwards Archbishop of Dublin (†1298), wrote on the first book
of the Sentences, on the unity of forms, and on the immediate
vision of the Divine Essence.   Thomas de Sutton attempted
a concord of the books of St. Thomas, and commented on
Aristotelian Logic and the Psalter   John of St. Giles, the
friend of Grosseteste, who was already a Master in Theology
when he assumed the Dominican habit in the midst of a sermon
on poverty, was the first professor in the School of St. Edward.[53]
Maurice of England wrote a book of *Distinctiones* as an aid for
the composition of sermons.   One of the English Dominicans
wrote *postillae* on St. Paul, another on Isaiah, a third on
Ecclesiastes; two of them wrote to vindicate Aquinas against
attack, three English Dominicans composed a Biblical
Concordance.[54]   Nor should we forget Robert Bacon the
Dominican, obscured by the fame of his relative and namesake
Roger, or his friend Richard Fitzacker or Fishacre, commentator
on the Sentences.[55]

exegesis of the Sentences was the fruit of such lectures.   It is this
organization of studies which has led one writer to call St Dominic 'the
first minister of public instruction in Europe'.

[52] It was the Thomist doctrine that there was one form in the human
composition   Kilwardby's treatise on the origin and division of knowledge
has been styled 'the most important introduction to philosophy of the
Middle Ages'.

[53] Trivet, *Annales*, s a 1222.   Trivet says John was *Suavissimus
moralizator* and also *in arte medicinae expertissimus*: he had lectured
in Montpellier as well as at Paris.   Under 1223 Trivet mentions the resigna-
tion of the bishopric of Carlisle by Walter Mauclerck (some years after
he became bishop in that year) and his entry into the Order

[54] These concordances are still used, and still called *Concordantiae
Anglicanae*, Bémont, ibid   Mandonnet dates them 1250–75, and men-
tions John of Darlington as their chief composer.   On the work of the
Dominicans in Oxford see Rashdall, *The Friars Preachers v. the University*
(Oxford Historical Series, xvi, pp. 195 sqq), and Fletcher, *The Black Friars
in England*.   An interesting question, which cannot here be investigated,
is that of the influence of the Friars on the growth of colleges ; cf. Rashdall,
Mediaeval Universities, i. 487, and Little, *Grey Friars in Oxford*, p. 9

[55] See Addendum I, p. 77.

PART II

THE ENGLISH CONVOCATION

EARLY in the history of the Church we find the Metropolitans convoking and presiding over provincial councils of bishops. Before the twelfth century these assemblies are not purely ecclesiastical assemblies, laymen may attend, and lay matters may be transacted.[1] In the course of that century these assemblies acquire a specifically and exclusively ecclesiastical character.[2] 'The restoration of discipline is generally the object of their deliberations ; or their purpose may be the defence of the rights of the Church, which is increasingly engaged in struggles with the secular power.'[3] But their powers are generally inconsiderable. the centralization of the Church in the hands of the Papacy cannot admit of any great vigour in these assemblies.[4] Gratian lays it down—*Concilia sunt invalida ad diffiniendum et constituendum, non autem ad corrigendum. Sunt enim necessaria episcoporum concilia ad exhortationem et correctionem.*[5] In composition these councils are essentially as Gratian says, and as Eadmer also says of English councils in the time of the Conqueror,[6] *episcoporum concilia*, though abbots will also be present, along with other churchmen of importance such as archdeacons, deans, and

---

[1] Cf. Viollet, *op. cit.,* i 355-60 ; ii 354. Viollet remarks that the councils which enacted the *Treuga Dei* were of the nature of 'great popular assizes', which laymen and even women attended. The Anglo-Saxon polity hardly knows a distinction between the ecclesiastical council and the lay assembly.

[2] For the reasons of this development in England see Stubbs, *Constitutional History,* ii 178-80.

[3] Viollet, *op. cit.,* ii. 354.

[4] See Moller, *Lehrbuch der Kirchengeschichte,* ii. 286, 306. While the Pope acts as a check above, the cathedral chapters below (claiming to be an episcopal *presbyterium* and the representatives of the diocesan clergy) impose another limitation (ibid., p. 307).

[5] Quoted in Viollet, *op. cit.,* ii. 354   But the disciplinary power over bishops is disappearing in 1200, see Moller, *op. cit.,* ii. 306.

[6] Eadmer, *Hist. Nov.* 1. 6, in Stubbs, *Select Charters,* p. 82.

priors.[7]   Above these provincial synods we find larger synods from a number of provinces, and national synods from all the provinces in a country, below them we find (side by side with the episcopal chapter which represents or claims to represent the clergy of a diocese) a diocesan synod composed of the priests and even the deacons of a diocese.

By the end of the twelfth century provincial synods were almost becoming extinct   As the bishop declined in power and authority (partly because he took more interest in his lay fief than in his spiritual position, partly because he was ousted by the growth of the chapter and the archdeacon), so, too, did the archbishop ; and as his power declined, so the provincial synods, which he convoked, became more and more infrequent. Ceasing to 'find themselves' in regular synods, the provinces ceased to be living communities, and became mere aggregations of bishoprics.[8]   A revival, however, came in the beginning of the thirteenth century. In the first place an impulse to synodal activity may be said to have been given by three great synods of the whole Church—the Fourth Lateran Council in 1215, and the two Councils at Lyons in 1245 and 1274. The composition of these great councils is especially noteworthy.   A new step is taken when Innocent III, in summoning the Fourth Lateran Council, asks bishops to enjoin the chapters of churches, not only cathedral but others, to send their provost or dean *or other suitable men on their behalf*, since some things are to be treated which will specially pertain to chapters.[9] Here is representation in the highest assembly of the Church—representation, indeed, not of the community of the diocese, but at

[7] Viollet, *op cit.*, ii 354, Makower, *Constit. Hist. of the Church of England* (Eng trans.), p. 359.

[8] Hauck, *Kirchengeschichte Deutschlands*, iv. 17   The mediaeval communities naturally found their centre of unity and source of life in the courts in which they issued.   The shire is a community in and through the shire-court—the borough in and through the borough-court. Indeed we may say that the shire is the shire-court. the same word *comitatus* covers both.   The shire ceases to be a living community of persons, and sinks into a geographical expression as the shire-court decays.

[9] Labbe and Cossart, *Concilia*, xi. 1, 124   This may be regarded as the first germ of our *praemunientes* clause. Hefele, *History of Councils*, i. 21-2, says that deputies of chapters appeared in Councils as early as 516 (at the Council of Tarragona). But the Fourth Lateran Council marks a new epoch for the Middle Ages.

any rate of the community of the chapter.   Similarly in 1245
Innocent IV enjoins archbishops to bid their suffragans come
and their chapters to send *providi nuncii et fideles qui vice
ipsorum utile nobis consilium largiantur*;[10] and a similar
method is adopted by Gregory X in 1274 when he asks for
viri idonei from chapters of churches, both cathedral and
others.[11]   In the second place, the Fourth Lateran Council
expressly enjoins, in its sixth canon, the observance of the old
canonical custom of annual provincial synods to control ecclesiastical life and to secure the observance of ecclesiastical law.
' Let metropolitans with their suffragans omit not each year
to celebrate provincial synods, for the correction of excesses
and reformation of manners, especially in the clergy, and let
persons be appointed to investigate what needs correction and
reformation and to report to the metropolitan and his suffragans
and others in the next council, that they may proceed with
prudent deliberation and cause to be observed what they have
enacted, publishing their enactments in episcopal synods to be
celebrated yearly in each diocese.' [12]   Of itself the re-enactment
is of no great importance, and by itself it would not have
achieved much.   But the tendency of events made for the
revival of such synods   In Germany the comparative frequency of provincial synods from 1230 to 1310[13] is ascribed
by the historian of the German Church partly to the disuse
during the reign of Frederic II of synods called by the king,

[10] Ibid., xi. 1. 636.
[11] Ibid , xi. 1. 941.
[12] Ibid., p. 153.   The twelfth canon (pp. 163-5) is also important.   It
commands triennial chapters to be held in each kingdom or province
of abbots and priors who have not been accustomed to hold such chapters.
This refers to the Benedictine abbeys, who are here commanded to
modify their principle of local autonomy, and to conform to the Cistercian
model.   Only in England was the command obeyed. it was re-enacted
by the legate Otto in 1238 in a meeting of the Benedictine abbots at
London (Matt Paris, iii. 508-10) ; and chapters are recorded in 1225 (cf.
Dugdale, *Mon Angl* , I. xlvi) and in 1249 (Matt. Paris, vi 175 sqq.).   But
during the thirteenth century no representatives attend these meetings.
[13] Between 1230 and 1310 there is a provincial synod in one province
or other every second year ; between 1310 and 1400 there are only eight
or nine provincial synods in the whole of Germany.   In the province of
Mainz there are ten provincial synods from 1230 to 1310 : there are none
after 1310 during the whole of the fourteenth century   Hauck, *op. cit.*,
v. I. 137-43.

paitly to the example of the national synods held by papal
legates, especially Conrad of Porto.[14]   It must be noted, however, that these synods dwindle and disappear after 1310, and
that in their composition they piesent a close corporation of
bishops and other prelates.   As at Magdeburg, in 1261, bishops,
abbots, priors, archdeacons, and other prelates of churches
form the synod: there is very little trace of representation,[15]
and what iepiesentation we find is of chapters and abbeys and
not of diocesan cleigy   When we tuin to France we find
a development during the thirteenth century which deserves
especial notice.   It concerns the chapters of cathedrals.   The
legatine Council of Bourges in 1225 is the first stage of this
development.   Here we see the influence of papal pressure on
institutional development in the Church.   At this council the
legate Romanus put forward the papal demand, made in the
bull *Supra muros Jerusalem* (January 28, 1225), for prebends
in all conventual churches.   Proctors of chapteis had been
summoned, as the mattei obviously concerned chapters   But
the legate gave these proctors leave to depart, keeping only
bishops and abbots.   The proctors protested; they feared that
in their absence ('who were of greater prudence and expeiience,
and from their numbers more able to iefuse') he should hold
conference with each chapter severally, and not with all in
common, and so should determine something to the general
prejudice.   They expressed their surprise that he had not
made the proposal in their presence, as they were specially
concerned, and they warned him that, if some consented, there
would yet be no real consent in a matter which concerned all
(a refeience to the dictum in the *Institutes* afterwards quoted by

---

[14] Hauck, *op cit*, iv. 17, v. 1. 135-6
[15] Hauck, v. 1. 149, n 1, writes: 'Die Halberstadt-Stifter in Aschaf-
fenburg waren durch Bevollmachtigte vertreten, die *vice ac nomine
omnium* handelten   Es wird auch anderwarts so gewesen sein.'   In the
national and legatine synod at Wurzburg in 1287 each chapter and abbey
was to be represented by two proctors (ibid, v. 1. 172), and in *diocesan*
synods Siegfrid of Cologne introduced in 1280 representation, by one or
two proctors, of the members of chapters and collegiate churches (ibid.,
n. 2, cf. Labbe and Cossart, xi. 1. 1108).   In diocesan synods representatives of capitular clergy already appear in the twelfth century (Hauck, v.
1 172), and in the fourteenth century representatives of the ordinary
diocesan clergy begin to appear (ibid., p. 173)

Edward I), when all, subjects as well as their kings and princes, were ready to resist to the death.[16]

This meeting at Bourges is especially noteworthy for several reasons. In the first place, it shows a strong feeling of the chapters that they are a community with a common interest, which must be expressed by the common voice acting through representatives. The root idea of representation is clearly visible · the reference to the dictum *quod omnes tangit ab omnibus approbetur* is significant · the demand of the chapters reminds one of Edward I's substitution of consultation with the federated shire-communities for separate negotiations with the several shire-courts. In the second place, there is a close connexion between the French assembly and the first meeting in England of proctors of chapters in 1226 (not, as Stubbs says, 1225) · the same papal pressure was responsible for both, and the proceedings of the French assembly formed the model for those of the English. In the third place, this use of proctors is new and, as far as I know, unprecedented in France. It will not support the view, which it is used by Stubbs to support, that 'the procuratorial system had long been used in foreign churches' As far as I can discover, apart from one or two instances of representation of collegiate churches in German diocesan synods of the twelfth century, the first great instance of the use of proctors in clerical assemblies [17] appears in the summons of the Fourth Lateran Council quoted above. Finally, the general position of the chapter in the economy of the Church demands some consideration [18] Under the Carolingians the canons of cathedral

---

[16] See Walter of Coventry, ii 227 (cited in Stubbs, *Const Hist* ii. 207), and also Matt. Paris, iii 105–9, and the *Register of S. Osmund*, ii. 51–4. Not only do English writers pay heed to this assembly its proceedings were made the model of the English assembly held to answer the same papal demand in April, 1226. The papal demand was then refused *juxta formam responsionis in concilio apud Bituricas* (*Reg S Osmund*, ii. 51). For the proceedings of Bourges cf also Labbe and Cossart, *Conc.* xi. 1. 291–4.

[17] No doubt clerical proctors had appeared to represent their chapters or abbeys, in business at Rome that concerned the individual chapter or abbey, for some time past. But I am here speaking of joint representation of communities in a clerical assembly.

[18] See Hauck, *op. cit*, v. 1. 185–221; cf also Viollet, *op cit.*, ii 356, and on the English chapters Makower, *Const. Hist. of the Church of England*, § 37

chapters had been brought under the rule of a common life the common life had involved the allocation of separate revenues for its support the separate revenues had brought to the chapter first a share in the administration, and then a right of separate administration, of the properties from which they came　The chapter had thus by the thirteenth century developed into a corporation, owning property and electing its own members, of such as had *stallum in choro et votum in capitulo.*　As such it became practically independent of the bishop: it elected him; it imposed conditions on him at his election; it excluded him from its meetings; and it began to share with him control of the diocese.　Meeting twice a year in its general chapter (*capitulum generale*) it became the parliament, as it were, of the diocese.　The old *presbyterium* or synod of diocesan priests still subsisted as the 'folk-moot' of the diocese, but the real *presbyterium* was the permanent and powerful chapter.　The Pope, willing to check the bishops, fostered the chapter. he encouraged both its right to elect the bishop and its claim to consent to his acts.　The common life had indeed disappeared the daily chapter (*capitulum quotidianum*) for the reading of the rule and for edification had gone; the canons were scattered about, busy in divers offices, and 'vicars' took their place in the cathedral; but the power of the chapter general only grew.　It is this development which explains at once the summoning of representatives of the chapters by Innocent III, and the tone of the chapters at the Council of Bourges in 1225.[19]　Above all, the separate financial position of the chapter, its corporate ownership of a property of its own, will explain the need of its direct consultation when matters of finance arise.

---

[19] The history of the English Church seems to show the diocesan clergy in a stronger position.　We must remember that the English Church was peculiar in having a large number of monastic chapters which, as monastic, could hardly claim to represent the secular clergy.　In any case it is striking that in the final form of Convocation in the province of Canterbury two representatives of the ordinary clergy of each diocese sit side by side with one representative for the clergy of each chapter.　The protest of the Berkshire rectors in 1240, and the complaint of the beneficed clergy of the archdeaconries in 1255 that a tithe has been given without their being consulted, point the way to this development.

Gradually the use of proctors of the chapters becomes common in the provincial synods of the French Church. The position which the chapters have attained by the thirteenth century demands their presence. As a French commune is a collective seignory, so a chapter is, as it were, a collective prelacy: it stands in the ecclesiastical hierarchy by the side of the bishop or abbot. It is a corporation owning property, it is an elective body which imposes *Wahlkapitulationen* on its nominee, it is the equal, almost the successor, of the diocesan synod; in all three capacities it must be represented. The province of Reims shows the way. Here there is a peculiar development. 'The chapters of the province federate (1234–1428) and hold regular annual assemblies. These chapters wish to defend their rights and privileges against the archbishop and his suffragans, they wish to guarantee their common interests by union.'[20] In 1277 this produced a counter-confederation of the bishops. In a council of the province at Compiègne they protested against the 'damnable usurpations' of the chapters, and bound themselves into a confederacy to meet annually at Paris, with money contributions on behalf of the common cause.[21] It was perhaps through this struggle that the chapters gained an entry into the provincial council by the side of the prelates. Already in 1235 synods of the province at St. Quentin and at Compiègne are attended not only by bishops, but by proctors of all the cathedral chapters of the province; and the synods protest against the attacks of the king on the liberties of the province. It is attacks on the chapter which come first in their complaints. the king has outlawed a canon of Reims, he has seized the property and otherwise infringed the rights of the chapter of Soissons.[22] Here it is royal pressure, as in 1225 it was the pressure of the Papacy, which brings capitular representation to the front. Henceforth the chapters seem to form part of the provincial synod. In 1239 the acts of the provincial synod of Reims are dated *consentientibus nobis episcopis . . inter-*

[20] Viollet, *Histoire des institutions*, ii 356. Viollet does not mention the counter-confederation of the bishops.

[21] Labbe and Cossart, *Conc.* xi. i. 1031–2.

[22] Ibid, p. 501–3

veniente etiam consensu procuratorum capitulorum ecclesiarum cathedralium provinciae nostrae.[23] In 1271, when the Bishop of Soissons held a council during a vacancy of the see of Reims, the canons of Reims disturbed its proceedings, 'forbidding any suffragan to be present, when they had not been consulted, and had not given permission for a synod'[24] In 1287 the perennial quarrel of the clergy with the friars on the hearing of confessions led to a provincial synod of Reims, attended by proctors of cathedrals *and other collegiate churches*, in which the bishops were ordered to pay one-twentieth of their revenue, and chapters and rectors of parochial churches one-hundredth, to meet the expenses of their cause.[25]

In other French provinces the same development is to be seen. In the province of Narbonne in 1246 the archbishop promulgates the constitutions of a synod *assensu . . . suffraganeorum nostrorum et capituli nostri.*[26] Here the archiepiscopal chapter alone is mentioned, and it is mentioned as if it were on a level with the suffragans.[27] In 1255 the synod of Narbonne is attended by bishops, abbots, many archdeacons, precentors and other ecclesiastical persons.[28] Here there is no mention of any chapter; but in 1280 we hear of episcopal chapters, and not as in 1246 of the archiepiscopal chapter only. A chapter writes to inform the archbishop that it has elected a proctor to attend the synod 'to hear discussion of business touching the whole province, and to do what seems good to the synod', and that it will hold firm and valid whatever the

---

[23] Labbe and Cossart, *op cit.*, xi. 1. 569   [24] Ibid., p. 922

[25] Ibid., xi. 2. 1317-18. Whether the proctors of chapters were always present at synods of the province of Reims, or only attended on special occasions, I cannot say In 1304 (Labbe and Cossart, xi. 2 1493) there are only bishops present: in 1317 (ibid., 1625) the deans and chapters of cathedral churches attend through proper proctors. In 1326 (ibid, 1769) proctors of cathedral churches are present, and on the whole their presence seems to be the rule.

[26] Ibid, xi. 1. 677.

[27] This form I have also noticed in the German Church at Cologne. In 1310 the archbishop promulgates statutes *de capituli et praelatorum nostrorum consilio et assensu* (Labbe and Cossart, xi. 2. 1517); and again in 1324 he enacts *de consilio et consensu nostri capituli Coloniensis ac venerabilium patrum* (ibid., p. 1708). Here the archiepiscopal chapter comes before the bishops of the province.

[28] Labbe and Cossart, xi 1. 753.

proctor shall do.[29]   Again in 1299 pioctois of chapters attend
a synod of the Narbonne piovince.[30]   A synod of 1374
especially deserves attention   The archbishop had been
armed by a letter and three bulls from Giegory XI, authorizing him to summon even exempt abbots and prelates to the
synod.   Accordingly he addressed a summons to his suffragans
(1) enjoining their attendance; (2) commanding them to
summon to attend in person all clergy who of use, custom, or
law, ought to attend in person, and to summon chapters,
colleges, and convents to attend through proctors, syndics, or
oeconomi, appointed for the purpose, with sufficient and special
mandate ; and (3) ordering them to hold diocesan synods to
deliberate in advance on the business of the provincial synod.
The synod was held : its constitutions are promulgated in
the following teims.   ' We the aichbishop, the bishops present,
the proctors of the absent bishops, with our venerable chapter
of Narbonne, celebrating a provincial council . . . with proctors
also of others our venerable chapters absent, of abbots, chapters,
priors, colleges, and many other ecclesiastics, exempt and
non-exempt, even fiiars, and of other oideis whatsoever of oui
province, ordain . . ' and so forth [31]   This summons seems
almost parallel to Peckham's summons of the ' Model Convocation' of 1283, though it is perhaps a uniquely laige
assembly.   Heie, as everywheie else, the one thing that
diffeientiates the churches of the Continent from those of
England is the absence of proctors of the diocesan clergy.
Nor is there, apparently, any such regular rule or ' canon '
deteimining the composition of provincial synods in France

[29] Ibid , p 1126   In 1279 the Archbishop of Narbonne had asked the
abbots, priors, chapters, and convents of his province to set their seal to a
power of attorney (*procuratorium*) authoizing him to treat at a parliament ' in France' about fiefs, arrière-fiefs, alods, the army, and other
grievances which touched the common state of the monasteries and
churches (ibid., p 1062).

[30] Ibid , xi 2. 1430.

[31] Ibid , pp. 2493–9.   One notices that the chapter of the archbishop is
mentioned apart from other chapters, and along with the archbishop and
his suffragans (as if *all* its members attended): it forms part as it were of
the inner ring, as apparently before in 1246   The phrase *proctors,
syndics, oeconomi* is apparently borrowed from the royal chancery.
Philip IV in 1302 summoned *ecclesiarum urbiumque oeconomos syndicos
et procuratoi es.*

as that of 1283 in England. In the province of Tours, for instance, chapters are summoned in 1294;[32] in 1315 the preamble of the constitutions of another synod runs—'those having been summoned who ought to be summoned, and those being present who wished or were able to be present, we have ordained by the counsel and consent of our suffragans and abbots.'[33]

On the whole, we may lay it down that the presence of representatives of chapters in provincial synods was common in France by the fourteenth century.[34] We must remember that by 1302 the meetings of the States General had begun To these meetings chapters were summoned to send proctors by royal letters addressed directly to the dean and chapter.[35] The parochial clergy, not possessing temporalities or jurisdiction, were not summoned either in person or through proctors.[36] The chapters, collective seignories as well as collective prelacies, enter the States General as well as the provincial synod · the ordinary clergy attend neither. In Spain, also, in the fourteenth century, proctors of chapters attend provincial synods. They are present in the province of Toledo in 1302,[37] and a council of 1324 definitely enacts, in order that fuller information may be had, that chapters of cathedral churches shall send fit proctors informed of the state of their churches.[38] In Germany we have already seen that representation of any sort is not frequent. There are two proctors from chapters and abbeys

[32] Labbe and Cossart, *op cit*, p. 1395   [33] Ibid, p. 1617.
[34] In the province of Auch proctors of all chapters of cathedral and collegiate churches attend at Béziers in 1290 (Labbe and Cossart, xi. 2 1363), and again in 1315 (ibid, p. 1621). In the province of Arles a proctor of the dean and chapter of one cathedral, a proctor of the bishop, dean and chapter of another, and three proctors of cathedral churches attend in 1288 (ibid, p. 1336) At a joint synod of three provinces at Avignon in 1326 proctors of the chapters of the provinces appear (ibid, p. 1719).
[35] Viollet, *op cit.*, iii 187-8.
[36] Stubbs, *Const. Hist.* ii. 180, n. 2, 210, n 2. Exceptionally the whole clergy of a diocese, regular and secular, may join to elect their deputies, as at Bourges in 1308, but only the important dignitaries attend; all the clergy of the diocese are not summoned—that would be too slow and costly, Viollet, *op. cit*, iii. 188
[37] Labbe and Cossart, xi. 2 2445
[38] Ibid., p. 1714

at the legatine Council at Wurzburg in 1287 , the chapter of
Cologne acts along with the suffragans in the synods of the
province in 1310 and 1324 ; the Archbishop of Cologne enacts
in 1280 that proctors of chapters and collegiate churches shall
attend diocesan synods, and in the fourteenth century diocesan
synods begin to include representatives of the ordinary clergy.
But on the whole 'the bishops and prelates of ecclesiastical
provinces acted in the provincial synods as an exclusive
corporation '.[39]   The constitutional development of the provincial organization of the Church went further in France than
elsewhere on the Continent; but it went no further than
representation of the cathedral clergy.   A study of the proceedings in the different churches at the time of the Council
of Vienne (1311) for the suppression of the Templars gives us
interesting results.   In the first place, the Pope does not
summon, as in 1215, 1245, and 1274, representatives of the
chapters to the general council; he summons from each
province the archbishop and a number of the bishops to
represent the whole province.[40]   In the second place, we may
notice in the different provincial synods which are held in 1310
to prepare the way for the general council some interesting
differences.   In England Winchelsea summons to London the
ordinary representative convocation (including proctors of
cathedrals and of the diocesan clergy).[41]   Other synods are
held for Italy, Spain, Germany, and France in the provinces
of Ravenna, Toledo, Mainz, and Sens.   At Ravenna there
attend bishops, two Dominicans and a Franciscan who are
inquisitors in the province, a rural dean for the *sacrati viri* of
Modena, a prior for the bishop and *sacrati viri* of Parma [42]
In the province of Toledo bishops attended ,[43] and at Sens
and Mainz bishops also apparently formed the council
Here we find councils in England, Italy, Spain, France, and
Germany; but in England alone do we find meeting a real
and regularly organized representive body.

We turn to the provincial synod of Canterbury and York,

[39] Hauck, *op. cit.*, v. I. 149
[40] Labbe and Cossart, xi 2   1507, 1543.
[41] Ibid , pp. 1511–12.   [42] Ibid., p. 1533
[43] Ibid., p. 1535.

and to the history of our own Convocation. Before 1226 there is no representative element in these synods. In 1207, when John attempted to exact from the clergy a tax on their spiritualities, it was to bishops and abbots only that he put forward the demand. There were no representative members at the assembly of 'religious' on which John imposed a heavy fine in 1210.[44] The assembly at St. Paul's in 1213, at which Stephen Langton produced the charter of Henry I, contained bishops, abbots, priors, and deans.[45] In 1225 Stephen Langton cites bishops, abbots, priors, deans, and archdeacons.[46] Only in 1226, five years after the settlement of the Dominicans in England, does Stephen Langton at last summon not only bishops, abbots, priors, deans, and archdeacons, but also proctors from each chapter of cathedral and prebendal churches and monasteries and other religious and collegiate houses, who are all to attend with full instructions.[47] Abbots, priors, and deans are no longer to come alone, we perceive, but each is to bring a *socius* from the body of which he is head, just as the conventual priors in the Dominican Order came to the provincial chapter each accompanied by a representative of his chapter. From 1226 we may leap forward to the beginning of the reign of Edward I. A Dominican, Kilwardby, once provincial prior of his Order, is now on the throne of Canterbury. In 1273 he summons not only capitular, but also

---

[44] *Venerunt . . ad hanc generalem convocationem abbates, priores, Templari Hospitalarii custodes villarum ordinis Cluniacensis.* Matt. Paris, p. 230, in Stubbs, *Select Charters*, p. 274

[45] Matt Paris, p 240, in Stubbs, *Select Charters*, p. 277

[46] Wilkins, *Concilia*, i. 558. The archdeacons may be regarded as representative of the diocesan clergy, and the deans of the capitular clergy. The representative character of the former is sometimes definitely emphasized. In 1258 the archdeacons were summoned with letters procuratorial from their clergy (Stubbs, *Select Charters*, p. 454); and in 1240 we find archdeacons prominent. In that year the legate associated with the Papal collector Petrus Rubeus summons the bishops to ask for money. The bishops say, 'We have archdeacons subject to us, who know the means of the beneficed clergy subject to them: we do not. *Omnes tangit hoc negotium · omnes igitur sunt conveniendi: sine ipsis nec decet nec expedit respondere.*' The bishops *and archdeacons* then meet to give a reply to the legate (Matt. Paris, iv. 37) The clerical use of the argument *quod omnes tangit* reminds us of the assembly at Bourges in 1225.

[47] Wilkins, *Concilia*, i. 602, quoted in Stubbs, *Select Charters*, p. 453

diocesan clergy, not only some greater persons from each chapter, but also proctors of all the clergy of each diocese.[48] The archdeacon now brings his *socius* also. The last step of all is taken by Peckham, a Franciscan friar, who summons the Model Convocation of the province of Canterbury in the year 1283. Bishops, abbots, priors, and other heads of religious houses, deans of cathedral and collegiate churches, and archdeacons are all to appear in person or by proctors; and the bishops are to assemble and instruct their diocesan clergy, so that from each diocese two proctors in the name of the clergy, and from each chapter of cathedral and collegiate churches one proctor, may be sent with sufficient instructions, having full and express power of treating and consenting.[49] Dean and archdeacon now both appear with their *socii*, who are proctors with full power; the evolution is complete. In York the evolution is slightly different here each archdeaconry sends two proctors, and here the Model Convocation is as early as 1280.[50]

It would be absurd to suggest that this evolution is entirely due to imitation of the Dominican model. It is only suggested that it is significant that the first step should have been taken by Langton, the friend of the Dominicans, and that the final steps should have been taken by two friars, the one belonging to the Dominican, the other to the Franciscan Order, in which the Dominican system had been adopted and in which the provincial chapters were composed of *custodes* each accompanied by a *discretus* elected by all the friars of the convent. But if the institutions of the friars perhaps supplied a model, there must have been some motive force which impelled the Church to the adoption of that model. And this motive force may be found in the need of meeting the demands which both the Papacy

---

[48] Wilkins, *Concilia*, ii. 30, quoted in Stubbs, *Select Charters*, pp 455-6. Representatives of the diocesan clergy had attended before, as we shall see, in the period 1254-8.

[49] Wilkins, *Concilia*, ii. 93, quoted in Stubbs, *Select Charters*, p. 467.

[50] Stubbs, *Const Hist.* ii. 207. But there are difficulties about this assembly of 1280, and I am not quite sure that it can be regarded as a model; cf. *infra*, p. 65 and note 132. In any case the assembly met in 1280, and not in 1279 (though it was summoned in that year), and Stubbs's date (1279) must therefore be altered.

and the English Crown made on the Church during the reign of Henry III, and which the Crown still continued to urge in the reign of Edward I.

The English Church in the reign of Henry III was in a somewhat peculiar position. The Pope was twice overlord of England, once as spiritual head of the Church, and once as temporal overlord since John's submission. This double power was used, already in the pontificate of Honorius III, and still more under his successor Gregory IX, to make England a milch-cow. On the plea of a Crusade taxes were imposed, intended for clergy and laity alike, but falling in the issue on the clergy, while under the shadow of his right of *provisio* [51] (and especially of the provision exercised *jure praeventionis*, which included reservations and expectatives) the Pope had begun to interfere with patronage and prebends. *Rex . . . factus est baculus arundineus*, as Matthew Paris more than once says. the clergy found that they were like sheep given over to ravening wolves with the king's connivance. Henry preferred sharing with the Pope to defending the Church; and the Church was thrown on itself. It had to reply as a whole, through some organized representation of itself, to the demands which first the Pope, then the Pope and king, and finally under Edward I the king by himself were constantly making. The principle *quod omnes tangit ab omnibus approbetur* already alleged in France in 1225, and urged in England in 1240, had to receive its full expression.

We may first study the illustration given by the events of the years 1225 and 1226. Early in 1225, on February 2, a council at London had granted a fifteenth of all movables *praeterquam de ecclesiis*, in return for a confirmation of the charters. [52] Honorius III had apparently been approached by the king beforehand, and at the same time, February 3, he wrote to the English Church, commanding that it should pay a competent subsidy according to the means of its churches. [53]

---

[51] See Stubbs, *Const. Hist* III. 313 sqq , and especially p 320, n. 1.

[52] Walter of Coventry, ii. 256 , Matt. Paris, III 91–2.

[53] Walter of Coventry, II. 256–7. The letter is also printed from the Salisbury Register in Wilkins, *Concil.* 1 603–4.

In the same year two other matters drew the attention of the Pope to England Fawkes de Breauté had appealed to him, and he sent a nuncio, Otto, with letters of intercession on his behalf.[54] But Otto was also the bearer of other letters. He brought the bull of January 28, 1225, *Supra muros Jerusalem*, in which a demand was made for one prebend in each cathedral and collegiate church, and for a certain revenue from all religious houses—the bull which the legate Romanus had put before the French Church at Bourges. The English Church had thus to face two demands from Honorius, one for a subsidy for Henry, another for contributions to the Papal See. Early in 1225 (the letter is not dated) Stephen Langton sent a letter to all the bishops, warning them to induce their clergy to grant an aid, according to the papal command, from the sources on which the fifteenth had not been levied, and so to make a virtue of necessity.[55] Nothing, however, seems to have been done in 1225, whether owing to the reluctance of the bishops to act, or to the coming of the nuncio, which may have suggested that they should wait for the results of his mission. At the end of 1225, however, Stephen sent a summons to his suffragans to come to London on the morrow (? octave) of Epiphany, January 7 (? 13), 1226, with their deans and archdeacons and with abbots and priors of convents.[56] The business was the discussion of the demands made in the bull *Supra muros Jerusalem*. The king, however, was lying ill at Marlborough, and the archbishop and several of the bishops were absent. The council accordingly, through the mouth of the archdeacon of Bedford, replied that in their absence they could not and ought not to give any answer on a matter that touched the king, all patrons of churches, and

---

[54] Walter of Coventry, ii. 272-4.

[55] Ibid., p 257; Wilkins, i. 603-4

[56] Matt. Paris, iii 102-3 , Wilkins, i. 558, 602, 603 Matthew Paris dates the council on the Feast of St. Hilary, which is the octave of Epiphany, and that is the date in Wilkins, i. 558 (January 13) But in Wilkins, i. 602, and the *Reg. S. Osmund*, ii. 46, the date given is the morrow of Epiphany.

[57] Stephen had gone to see the king at Marlborough (Wilkins, i. 559; *Register of St Osmund*, ii. 45), perhaps to concert a policy with the king and his advisers in the face of Otto.

innumerable prelates. Otto sought to fix a time for another meeting, but he failed to secure the consent of the council. The failure of this council led to the summoning of a new council, in which representation was adopted on the model of the council at Bourges the year before   Stephen sent a new summons, which was received at Salisbury at the beginning of March   Not only were bishops, abbots not exempt, priors, deans, and archdeacons to attend ; but each chapter was to send proctors, as well of cathedral as of prebendal churches and of monasteries and other religious and collegiate houses, to be present, to deliberate and to come fully instructed to answer the legate   The meeting was fixed at London for April 26. In the interval Stephen had been active. He had procured from Rome letters recalling Otto : while the nuncio was travelling North in Lent (Easter Day in 1226 fell on April 19), he received the letters at Northampton, read them askance, threw them into the fire, and left England in confusion with his wallet empty.[58] We can now understand the absence of Stephen from the council of January , he had been negotiating with Honorius. The letters he had obtained from Honorius commanded him to summon a new council and therein to gain an answer himself to the papal demand. This will explain the new summons received at Salisbury at the beginning of March , and it is thus to Stephen's initiative that we must ascribe the introduction of the representative principle in that summons. Once more Stephen shows himself a father of English liberty. And we should notice in passing the wide scope of the representation he introduces . it is representative not only of chapters, as at Bourges, but of monasteries and

[58] This is Wendover's account (Matt. Paris, iii. 109). I must admit that Walter of Coventry, in the last paragraph of the Memoranda, contradicts this account. He speaks of the nuncio Otto as present at the meeting at London, which he dates not on April 26, but fifteen days after Easter (i. e May 4, not April 13, as Stubbs says in the side-heading, an error repeated in *Const. Hist* ii. 39), and as reciting the bull *Supra Muros*. Not many days after the council the nuncio receives papal letters and leaves England (i. e towards the end of May). But this last paragraph is not found in MS A , and the *Register of St. Osmund*, ii. 51, corroborates Wendover (*Octone versus curiam Romanam profecto, tenuit dominus Cant. concilium*).

other religious houses.[59] The example of Bourges must have weighed with Stephen;[60] but is it a risky conjecture that he was also influenced by his friends the Dominicans, and that he partly borrowed from their organization this use of representatives of religious houses, in which, one fancies, representatives of Dominican convents may have been themselves included ?[61]

When the representative council met at London at the end of April, 1226,[62] it returned a *non possumus* to the papal demands. 'The demands of the Pope look to the whole breadth of Christianity · we, situated as we are on the extreme confines of the world, will see how other realms behave towards such demands : when we have done so, and have an example from other realms, the Pope will find us prompter in obedience.' The king, fearing for his own interests, had on this question opposed the Papacy.[63] But there was still to be settled the

[59] The papal bull demanded prebends in cathedral and prebendal churches, and from monasteries and other regular houses and collegiate churches revenues according to their means   Stephen follows exactly the wording of the bull (cf. Walter of Coventry, ii. 275, and Wilkins, 1 558, with Wilkins, i. 603)   It is not so much of his own initiative, as in exact obedience to the wording of the bull, that he goes beyond the French precedent of 1226   But at any rate he sees that if the bull is to be answered by means of representation, the representation must be as wide as the demands of the bull ; and the addition of monastic to capitular representatives makes his assembly far wider than that at Bourges

[60] The proceedings of Bourges were apparently read before the English assembly when it met, *Reg. St Osmund*, ii 51 , cf. *supra*, n 16.

[61] Mr A G Little, who has been kind enough to read through this study, reminds me (1) that according to Trivet, *Annales*, s a. 1230, the provincial chapters of the Dominicans in England began in 1230 , (2) that Dominicans, vowed to poverty, could hardly have attended an assembly like that of 1226, which dealt with questions of property.   I would only urge, as touching the first point, that Langton may well have heard from his Dominican friends about the system on which the chapters, and especially the general chapters, of their Order were organized abroad, even if that system was not yet operative in England.

[62] We should notice the date, 1226. Stubbs, in taking the summons from Wilkins, i. 603, wrongly dates it 1225   Wilkins heads his excerpts from the Salisbury Register with the date 1225 ; but the only document to which that date applies is the first.   All the other documents must be dated (in our reckoning : Wilkins' year began on March 25) in 1226. A comparison with Matt. Paris makes this absolutely clear

[63] He had sent John Marshall and others to the abortive assembly at London in January, 1226, to tell all the prelates who held baronies of the king in chief not to bind their lay fief to the Church of Rome, whence he would be deprived of his service due (Matt. Paris, iii. 103).   The papal bull had demanded *de bonis episcoporum, secundum facultates suas . . . certi redditus* (Walter of Coventry, ii. 275)

matter of the competent subsidy to the king from churches, of which Honorius had spoken in his letter of February 3, 1225. Nothing apparently had been done towards its payment, and the king could now exert the more pressure, as he had apparently defended the Church in the other and greater matter. Here the Register of Salisbury gives us interesting information.[64] On Tuesday, June 16, 1226, the dean and chapter of Salisbury received a letter from their bishop, with two enclosures—the first the old letter from Stephen Langton, belonging to 1225, which recites Honorius's letter of February 3, demanding an aid for Henry, and suggests the making a virtue of necessity , and the second another and recent letter, in which Stephen recalls to memory (*a memoria vestra non credimus excidisse*) the proceedings of 1225, and suggests a twelfth or at least a fourteenth from these sources on which the fifteenth had not been levied. On the same day the dean and chapter also received a letter from the king, dated May 27, in which he recites how the Pope had lately (*dudum*) written to the English Church on his behalf, asks for an efficacious aid, and mentions that he has conceded to the Church, on the advice of Stephen and his bishops, tithes of hay and mills from his demesnes for the future. A chapter general attended by twenty-eight out of the thirty-seven canons was at once summoned to discuss (1) whether they should give the king an aid , (2) how it might be brought about, that one and the same form should be observed in divers churches (in other words, how, whether by use of representation or otherwise, the rate of the aid might be made uniform— an important point); (3) whether the rate should be one-twelfth or one-fourteenth ; and (4) how the creation of a precedent might be avoided. Thus the chapter constitutes itself a small parliament, to discuss parliamentary questions of

[61] The *Historia et acta capitulorum ecclesiae Sarum* (1217–28 · Wilkins, 1 551–69) and the excerpts from the Register dealing with 1226 (Wilkins, 1. 602–6) have been of great service. The *Register of St. Osmund* (Rolls Series) gives Stephen's two summons of Convocation (1 369–71, and also 11. 46–7 they are misdated by the editor in 1224 in the first volume, and vaguely dated 1225–6 in the second). The documents bearing on the proceedings of 1226 are in vol. 11, pp. 55-76.

representation and precedent. One feels that the leaven of Stephen's summoning of representatives earlier in the year is already at work. And the issue corroborates one's feeling. The meeting was held in the middle of August : the issue was a letter addressed by the dean and chapter to their bishop. They desire that, for the sake of uniformity (Honorius had spoken in his letter of *congruae collectae*, and Stephen in his of *forma eadem in singulis dioecesibus*), from each church where clerks live in common a proctor should be summoned, that from their uniform provision and counsel a certain and uniform answer may proceed ; and they further desire a security from the king that anything now done be counted as no precedent. The Bishop of Salisbury submitted the letter to Stephen Langton, and was able to reply, in a letter received by the chapter on September 8, that he had induced the archbishop to consent that each chapter should be allowed to send a proctor to London to a meeting on October 13, and that he commanded them to send one.[65] The chapter at once elected not one, but two proctors. The two proctors carried to London a letter from the chapter to Stephen, in which it promised to hold valid whatever the two proctors together with the proctors of other chapters thought proper to do. The two proctors further received from the chapter eleven articles of instruction. These articles are of great interest. The chapter thinks (§ 1) that it is proper to help the king—if the proctors of other chapters are of the same opinion ; but it thinks a twentieth (such as is given for the Holy Land) will be adequate (§ 2). This twentieth should be given on the basis of the assessment made before for the contribution (of 1219) in aid of the Holy Land (§ 4), and on prebends and revenues, not on movables ; it should be collected by trustworthy men, assigned by the chapter itself (§ 5). The proctors should inquire what is to be done if any of the canons singly contradict what has been provided by the majority of the chapter—which raises the interesting question of the right of a majority (§ 9). We

---

[65] Whether Stephen's action was as much due to the influence of Salisbury as would here appear we cannot say. Other chapters may have made the same request.

gather the issue of the meeting to which these proctors went
from a letter sent by Stephen Langton to the Bishop of
Salisbury towards the end of October. He had treated, so
he wrote, with the deans who were present, and with proctors
where deans were not present ; with the archdeacons present,
and the proctors of those who were absent ; [66] and with monks
present and the proctors of monks who were absent. They
had granted a sixteenth on all sources not touched by the
fifteenth of the previous year   it was given on the basis of the
old assessment of the twentieth for the Holy Land, and it was
to be collected by the dean and chapter in cathedral churches.
We see that the proctors of Salisbury have carried out some
of the articles of their instructions   The account in the
Register of Salisbury ends with a letter from the king, in
which he promises to make no precedent of the grant, and
a letter from the dean and chapter to their *concanonicus* N.,
asking for his contribution to the sixteenth [67]

The developments which mark these years are closely connected with the history of taxation. The papal demand, as
far as I know new and unprecedented, for prebends from
chapters and contributions from other ecclesiastical corporations, produces the new and unprecedented representation of
chapters both at Bourges in 1225 and at London in April 1226.
The royal demand, not altogether new and unprecedented as
a demand, but nevertheless new and unprecedented in its
particular character and in its success, produces representation
once more in England in October 1226   For what is touched
by the royal demand is the spiritualities of the clergy ; and
though kings have before sought to tax spiritualities, the
attempt of 1225-6 is in reality of a new kind. The Saladin
tithe had touched spirituality, but the Saladin tithe was *in
sustentationem terrae Hierosolymitanae* ; the ransom of Richard

---

[66] The difference of phrase is significant : *cum decanis . . . praesentibus,
et cum procuratoribus ubi decani non erant praesentes, cum archidiaconis
praesentibus et cum procuratoribus absentium.*

[67] In writing to their fellow canon the dean and chapter say that they
have received letters from Stephen Langton saying that an assembly at
London of deans or their proctors, archdeacons or their proctors, and
monks or their proctors has granted a sixteenth. The phrase is loose   it
does not reproduce Stephen's letter accurately   (Wilkins, i. 606.)

had involved taxation of spiritualities, but the ransom of a crusading king is an exceptional case. The frontal attack of the secular power on spiritualities in 1207 had failed; and the years 1225 and 1226 first offer an instance of taxation of clerical spiritualities (for the sixteenth of 1226 is paid from goods which had not paid the fifteenth of 1225, and these must be spiritualities), in which the taxation is actually levied by the lay power—it is true with papal assent—for lay objects. It is therefore in reality a demand of a new kind which produces the second representative assembly of the clergy in 1226.[68]

The events of the year 1226 are thus of great importance in the history of the development of procuratorial representation of the clergy. Twice representative assemblies appear— on April 26, to answer the papal demand for prebends; on October 13, to answer the other demand for an aid for the king.[69] A long step has been taken towards the evolution of a representative Convocation. It has been taken by Stephen Langton, once more as in 1215 the friend of English liberty. Whether or no we are justified in seeing the result of Dominican influence is an insoluble question, but that influence is at any rate a possibility. At any rate the canons of Salisbury have shown a clear grasp of the idea of a community and of representation as the means of uniform action of a community: they have even raised the question of majority rule. Is not this year 1226 after all more important in the genesis of representation than 1213? John certainly summoned in 1213 four men (not knights, as is often erroneously said) to talk with him at Oxford on the business of

[68] The sixteenth would affect diocesan clergy as well as capitular; but only the capitular clergy are represented in the assembly which votes the tax A precedent had been set for their representation earlier in the year; and the precedent is exactly followed, though it should properly have been extended further. That extension comes in 1254, as we shall see, when the Crown is demanding an aid, and when, summoning knights from shire-courts, it summons *pari passu* clergy from diocesan synods.

[69] As far as I can see, Stubbs makes two slips about the aid. (1) He speaks of it as having been granted twice, in 1225 and 1226, though he adds in a footnote that the one was the same as the other (*Const. Hist.* ii. 183). (2) He says 'probably the grant was made in diocesan synods' (ibid., n 3) It was made in a general assembly of the Church, as he really himself indicates on p. 39, n. 2.

his kingdom; but we know nothing of their meeting, if indeed they ever met. Earlier in the same year he had either summoned four men and the reeve from each vill on royal demesne to St. Albans, or (as Mr. Turner thinks) he had summoned four men and the reeve from each vill on episcopal demesne, or (as Mr. Davis thinks) he had instructed the sheriffs, without giving them time to execute his instructions, to convene four men and the reeve from each vill on royal demesne to shire-court to give information which the sheriffs were to bring to St. Albans In any case the only question was one of a jury of recognition to give evidence on the losses of the bishops since 1208.[70] But the events of 1226 are surely far more important in the history of representation than those of 1213. And the lesson they teach is that of the influence of the clergy on progress in political ideas. That is just the lesson we should expect to find in history. As Viollet says, ' Le clergé se trouva, du premier jour, habitué et comme rompu à ce que nous appellerions aujourd'hui les usages parlementaires.'[71] They had experience of assemblies: they had experience of representative *procuratores* the new Orders, constantly experimenting and advancing, as we have seen, had widened and deepened that experience It seems paradoxical to go beyond Bishop Stubbs in exalting clerical influence · yet when he contents himself with drawing only analogies between clerical and secular assemblies, and with stating that ' the practice of representation appears nearly at the same time in the Church Councils and in the parliaments,'[72] he really understates the

[70] See, for Mr Turner's view, *Eng. Hist. Rev.* xxi. 297–9, and for the view of Mr. Davis, ibid., xx. 289–91. I confess I am convinced by Mr Turner: the natural assembly to determine the losses and compensation of the bishops is an assembly recruited from men who live on episcopal estates. I may add that I am tempted to bring into connexion with the assembly of 1213 the entry in the *Waverley Annals*, p. 260, under the year 1208 (Stubbs, *Select Charters*, p. 274) John's commissioners in 1208 had seized the goods of the clergy movable and immovable, and had entrusted their care in each vill to men of the vicinity, at whose hands the clergy should receive from their goods what they absolutely needed What more natural than that inquiry should be made about the losses of the bishops from those men of the vicinity in each vill in which episcopal property lay?

[71] *Histoire des institutions de la France*, ii 355.

[72] *Const. Hist.* ii 204

case for the clergy.[73]   He attached too much weight in comparison to the old communal institutions of England, such as
the attendance of the four men and the reeve at hundred and
shire-court, and to the influence of the judicial procedure of
Henry II.   But though the jury of Henry II may contain
a form of representation, it is representation merely to give
information (*ad recognoscendum*), and not to take action (*ad
faciendum*).   The jurors are picked, often perhaps more or less
at random, as samples of the *publica fama* whose voice the king
and his justices would fain hear, much as the *miles argentarius*
picked 44 shillings from the sheriff's quota for weighing, and
20 from those 44 for assay, as samples of the whole.   Representatives who are proxies for their constituents, to determine
a course of action on their behalf, are a different matter ;
they demand as their vital atmosphere a mode of thought
and a set of ideas in which conceptions like *procuratorium*,
the binding of constituents by representatives, and further of
minorities by majorities, are consciously realized.   Only the
clergy can give that atmosphere of thought and ideas.   After
all, the creative political thought of the Middle Ages is
clerical . the clergy create the thought of monarchy proper as
opposed to mere feudal suzerainty ,[74] they create or recreate
the Holy Roman Empire ; they create the Crusade as an idea
and an institution.   May we not hold, in the light of our
evidence, that they go far to create representation ?[75]

[73] Cf. also p 210, n 3 : 'Although the procuratorial system as used in
clerical assemblies has a certain bearing on the representative system in
England, it is much less important here than in [other] countries. . . . In
England the two forms grow side by side, the lay representation is not
formed on the model of the clerical '

[74] Cf. Luchaire, *Histoire des institutions monarchiques sous les premiers
Capétiens*, vol. 1, *ad init.* (on the meaning of the elevation of Hugh Capet
in 987, which he interprets as *un fait ecclésiastique*).

[75] Before leaving the year 1226, I may perhaps correct an error in
Makower, *Const. Hist. of the Church of England*, p. 359.   He dates the
use of representation in the Scotch Church from 1225.   This would be
important if it were true.   But the document which he cites to prove the
attendance of *capitulorum collegiorum et conventuum procuratores idonei*,
in 1225, is a letter of Thomas Innes to Wilkins in 1735 (Wilkins, i,
p. xxx).   Now Innes does say that the Scotch Church legislated to this
effect in 1225 ; but if we turn to the documents of 1225 themselves,
printed in Wilkins (i 608), we find that bishops, abbots, and priors form
the council, though any of them may send a proctor on his own behalf if

But we must turn to the further history of the development.
The principle of clerical representation in 1226 was incomplete.
Stephen Langton had only summoned proctors from clergy
living a common life, in chapters, monasteries, and collegiate
churches ; he had not summoned representatives of the ordinary
diocesan clergy.   After his death, though the peculiar conditions of the English Church in the time of Henry III involve
a frequent and almost annual activity of the synods, the use of
representation does not for some time make any considerable
progress   Langton had died in 1228 , his next three successors, Richard le Grand, Edmund Rich, and Boniface of Savoy,
however different from one another in character, were none of
them made of his strong stuff.   In 1237, indeed, we find the
legate Otto using the idea of procuration to some extent at
a legatine council in London.[76]   The legate, who may have
remembered the history of the proceedings during his previous
visit in 1226, ordered archbishops, bishops, abbots, and priors
to come as well in the name of their convent or chapter as in
their own, bringing procuratorial letters, so that the enactments
of the council should be held valid on both sides , and the
council, thus composed, 'passed canons which form an epoch
in the history of our ecclesiastical jurisprudence.'[77]   Still a
further step was taken during his visit in 1240, when, as has
already been mentioned above,[78] the bishops replied to a
demand for money by urging the necessity of the presence of
the archdeacons who were acquainted with the means of their
beneficed clergy, and actually gained their point.   Here the
archdeacons appear as in some sense representatives of the
ordinary diocesan clergy, and some progress is made towards
the inclusion of diocesan with capitular clergy in a representative scheme.   The pressure of taxation already drives the
clergy further along the path of representation.[79]

he is hindered by any canonical impediment.   That, obviously, is quite
another matter

[76] Matt. Paris, ii. 415
[77] Tout, *Political History of England*, iii. 57.
[78] Note 46.
[79] In 1240 also falls the protest of the Berkshire rectors against papal
demands.

It is in 1254 that events begin to move fast.   In the State
as well as in the Church development appears.   Thirty years
of experience of the rule of Henry III are bearing fruit ; and
even if Boniface of Savoy is archbishop, the voice of the clergy
will out, and representation will come.   On February 11 of
1254 the regents, Eleanor and Earl Richard, summon for the
first time in our history [80] knights of the shire to a central
assembly.   The sheriff is to expound to the knights and
others of his shire the king's needs, and to induce them
thereby to pay a sufficient aid ; he is further to cause two
knights of the shire to be elected by the shire-court in lieu
of all and single of the shire, who, instructed by the sheriff's
exposition and by the consequent discussion in the shire-
court, will, along with other knights from other shires, be
able to answer precisely for their shire about the aid.   The
preliminary local discussion, in shire-court, and the instructions
given as a result to the shire-knights, remind us of the proceedings of the Salisbury chapter in 1226.[81]   It is important
to notice that the assembly, which in the issue proved fruitless,
probably also included representatives of the clergy of each
diocese [82]   This clerical representation is doubly important.
Here we have mentioned, for the first time, representatives of
the diocesan clergy , and here we see these representatives
meeting not in a separate clerical assembly, but in a national
parliament along with the knights of the shire.   In both points
the event is new and unprecedented.   In 1255 a further step
was taken.   At a parliament at Westminster after Michaelmas,
which included clerical proctors who were there *pro universitate*,
the king asked the clergy to grant an aid from their lay fiefs,
intending afterwards to extend the same demand to the laity.

[80] Not, as Stubbs and Professor Tout say, 'for the first time since the
reign of John' (*Const. Hist.* ii 69 and *Pol Hist.* iii 77).   John had not
summoned knights, but simply *homines*.

[81] Stubbs, *Select Charters*, pp. 376–7 ; *Const. Hist.* ii 69.

[82] In a writ of the same date, February 11, addressed to each bishop,
the regents ask for the convocation of diocesan synods, in which the
bishops are to induce the clergy to give an aid, and from which representatives are to come to certify the council of the aid granted   These representatives are to attend on the same day as the knights.   The writ is
printed in Hody, *History of Convocation*, Part III, p. 339.

The clergy present, including the proctors, sent their *gravamina* to the Pope, Alexander IV, whose predecessor, Innocent IV, had already in 1254 given the king a tithe from the English Church for two years.[83] The *Annals* of Burton quote the *gravamina* of the proctors of the beneficed clergy of the archdeaconry of Lincoln, who complain *pro tota communitate* of the grant of a tithe of their benefices to the king *ipsis non vocatis*; 'for especially, when it is a matter of binding any man, is his express consent necessary.' Similar articles were sent to the Pope from every diocese.[84] Here the clergy, attacked first by the king, naturally take the lead in emphasizing the principle of representation. Again in 1256, when an ecclesiastical assembly was convoked for January 18 to answer the demands of the nuncio Rustand, who had come in 1255 with power to collect the clerical tithe, there were summoned deans of cathedrals with discreet canons as proctors of their chapter, and archdeacons with three or four discreet clerks of their archdeaconries both on their own behalf and with procuratorial mandate for their fellows.[85] The business hung fire. Again on April 2 the nuncio published his instructions before an assembly of archdeacons, and it was settled that deans, prelates, regulars (? abbots) and archdeacons should treat with their chapters and clerks, so that they might return in the month after Easter to answer fully through instructed proctors.[86] Rustand, however, made no progress. In 1257 we again hear of a form of representation : Boniface of Canterbury summoned to a convocation in London, on August 22, deans of chapters and archdeacons with procuratorial letters in the names of their chapters and clergy.[87] Once more in 1258, when Rustand returned to the charge with a second nuncio, Boniface summoned a meeting to

---

[83] *Annales de Burton*, p. 325 ; cf. *infra*, n. 90.

[84] Ibid., pp. 360, 363. It should be noticed that representative clergy certainly attend the parliament of 1255 along with the laity—for the last time until 1282.

[85] Matt. Paris, vi. 315 ; Stubbs, *Const. Hist.* ii. 206 : Makower, *Const. Hist. of the Church of England*, p. 360. As Makower remarks, this is the first instance of representatives of inferior beneficed clergy in a clerical assembly. The assemblies of 1254 and 1255, in which such representatives had appeared, were not clerical.

[86] *Ann. de Burton*, p. 389.   [87] Ibid., pp. 401-2.

Merton for June 6, at which deans, abbots, priors, and archdeacons were to attend with procuratorial letters from their subject clergy, *propter ecclesiae Anglicanae eventus et causas.*[88] A few days later, June 11, 1258, the events of these four troubled years, 1254 to 1258, culminated in the Mad Parliament at Oxford. The whole realm was to undertake that reformation for which the clergy had been travailing, and the Mad Parliament was a full assembly of baronage and higher clergy with that object.

The years 1254 to 1258 are obviously a time of crisis, when development is rapid. In some respects they repeat the events of 1225 and 1226. There is a demand for taxation from the clergy for the use of the king; the demand is backed by the Pope, a papal nuncio is present. The combination of royal and papal pressure produces, in the one case as in the other, a demand for representation. In the one case, however, we only find representation of chapters; by 1258 we find representation of the beneficed clergy of the archdeaconries, which is used in 1254 and 1255 for joint assemblies of clergy and laity; in 1256 for a purely clerical assembly; and is again employed, in a lesser degree (the archdeacons having procuratorial letters from the clergy), in 1257 and 1258. The reason for the advance is plain. The demands of 1225 had primarily touched the capitular clergy; the later demands affected the ordinary beneficed clergy as well. Already in 1240 the papal demand for a tax on *all* clerical goods[89] to support the war against Frederic II, which began in 1239, had produced the protest of the Berkshire rectors and the refusal of the bishops to act unless the archdeacons were consulted. The war continued, and with it the papal exactions.[90] By 1254

---

[88] *Ann. de Burton*, pp 411–12; Stubbs, *Select Charters*, p. 454

[89] The first demand had already been made in 1229 by Gregory IX during the first war against Frederic II. Gregory had demanded a tenth from all movables, lay as well as clerical. The laity had refused; the higher clergy had consented, and the clergy had paid (except in Cheshire, where the earl refused to allow the clergy to do so). Matt Paris, III. 186–9

[90] These exactions are based on the theory that the war against the Emperor is a Crusade (see H. Pissard, *La Guerre Sainte en Pays Chrétien*, Paris, 1912, pp. 121 sqq) In 1215 it had been enacted at the Fourth Lateran Council (Labbe and Cossart, *Conc.* xi. 1. 220) that all

Henry had added to the burden in various ways   In 1250 he had taken the Cross, and been granted clerical tithes by the Pope on that ground for some years   In 1253 he had started an expensive campaign in Gascony, which led to the summoning of representatives in 1254.   It was a more serious matter that in 1254 he had dragged England into the papal war against the Hohenstaufen, by accepting Sicily for his son Edmund, and had thus at once imposed new burdens of his own on England, and given the Papacy a fresh excuse for pressing its exactions.   It is the cumulative effect of these events which explains the development between 1254 and 1258 ; and it is the fact that the taxes on the clergy, whether demanded by the Pope for himself or for the king, fell as heavily on the ordinary clergy of the dioceses as on other clergy, which explains their inclusion in the representative bodies convened to meet such demands   Whether any other influence than the pressure of taxation made for representation it is difficult to say.   The chief feature of the history of the Dominican Order between 1254 and 1258 is its struggle with the University of Paris.[91]   Simon de Montfort, friend of the Order, stiffened resistance in these years ; it was in the convent of the Order at Oxford that the Mad Parliament met in 1258.[92]   But if we are willing to regard clerical representation

clerks, *tam subditi quam praelati*, should pay one-twentieth of ecclesiastical revenues for three years, for the aid of the Holy Land, under pain of excommunication   (It is the assessment for this twentieth of which the canons of Salisbury speak in 1226.)   The twentieth became a tenth in 1229, when Gregory IX sought to extend it to the laity ; in 1240 it became even a fifth.   Innocent IV in 1245 at the Council of Lyons (Labbe and Cossart, *Conc.* xi I. 655) repeated the enactments of the Council of 1215 ; and in 1246 he demanded a half, a twentieth, and a third from different classes of the clergy (Stubbs, *Const. Hist* ii. 70).   In 1250 Henry III took the Cross , and Innocent IV, to attach him to the papal side, authorized him in 1251 to exact for his Crusade a tenth of the revenues of the clergy for three years on a new assessment (Stubbs, *Const Hist* ii. 67), and added a tithe for two more years in 1254, commuting at the same time the Crusade for the Sicilian enterprise.   For the further history of papal exactions in England see Stubbs, *Const Hist.* iii 346–9.   For a list of the exactions in the reign of Henry III see *Ann. de Burton*, pp 364–7

[91] This struggle, which lasted from 1252 to 1259, is noticed by Matthew Paris, iv. 416, 506, 528, 598, 645, 744, and by the *Ann. de Burton*, pp. 430–5 ; cf Rashdall, *op cit*, i 373 sqq

[92] Matt. Paris, iv. 697   Little (*Grey Friars*, p. 72, note), in mentioning

as at all a Dominican seed, sown by Stephen Langton, all we can say is that it was growing in this period.

In the troubled period of the Barons' War, with papal and royal exactions removed, clerical representation is not so prominent. Not even to Simon's great parliament of 1265, largely clerical as that assembly was, were clerical proctors summoned. Later in 1265, however, two proctors from each chapter were summoned, with full power of treating, to a parliament at Winchester on the first of June,[93] but as Prince Edward had escaped and begun to raise troops in May it can hardly have met. Not until 1273 do we again get a clear instance of clerical representation.[94] Why had de Montfort not incorporated clerical proctors in his parliament of 1265? Was it that they only came 'when the business specially touched the clergy', and there was no such business? Or was it that, with so great a majority of the higher clergy present (some 120, to 23 earls and barons) he was afraid to overweight the assembly with his clerical supporters? Whatever the reason, clerical representation ceases for the fifteen years 1258-1273, save for the dubious instance of 1265.

The parliament of 1265, in which clerical proctors did not appear, but representatives of the towns sat by the side of the knights for the first time in English history,[95] may here claim some attention. Simon's action in summoning representatives of towns has been explained by different writers as modelled

this fact, suggests that the Dominicans seem to have been royalist. The only evidence he adduces is that Friar John Darlington, one of the king's twelve on the committee of twenty-four, was a Dominican. This evidence is hardly sufficient for the suggestion; and the suggestion neglects the connexion of the Dominicans with de Montfort. On the other hand, Kilwardby in the next reign certainly seems more of a royalist than Peckham. See Addendum I, p 77

[93] Stubbs, *Select Charters*, p. 418.

[94] I am not clear about the meeting of 1269 (Wilkins, II. 20) (*Procuratores Coventr Linc Norwyc.* &c.) which Stubbs translates as 'proctors of the several dioceses' (*Const. Hist.* II. 206). The proctors may only have been proctors of absent bishops.

[95] The supposed instance of 1213 fades away on examination. If four men and a reeve had come from each vill on royal demesne, then (since villa includes town as well as township, and since most towns were on royal demesne) representatives of towns would have attended. But we have already seen reason to explain the passage in Matthew Paris otherwise.

on the institutions of Aragon, of Sicily, and of Gascony.[96]   It would seem absurd to add a fresh explanation, or to suggest the influence of the Church, and particularly of the friars, as a possible source.   We may, however, raise one or two considerations.   In the first place, de Montfort was closely connected with the friars.   St. Dominic had been closely associated with his father; Simon himself was perhaps the pupil of the Dominicans; his wife found a refuge, and a resting-place, in the house of the canonesses of St Dominic at Montargis.   His library contained at least one Dominican treatise.   He was also connected with the Franciscans through his friendship with Adam de Marsh and with the friend of the Franciscans, Robert Grosseteste.[97]   In the second place, the Song of Lewes,[98] generally attributed to a friar of the Franciscan Order, throws light on Simon's ideas on 'the government of soul and body', on which he had so often talked with Adam de Marsh and Grosseteste; and it deserves consideration alongside of the *Forma Regiminis* of 1264, to which Monsieur Bémont bids us look for Simon's political theory.   It illustrates the sentiments not only of the Franciscans but of the Universities, and not only of the Universities but of Simon himself, who had talked with those teachers of the Universities, Marsh and Grosseteste, from whom the doctrine of the Song was drawn.[99]   That the Song definitely suggests representation we can hardly say, the words

> *Igitur communitas regni consulatur*
> *Et quid universitas sentiat sciatur*

may refer only to the 'community of the prelates and barons' mentioned in the *Forma Regiminis* of 1264   Yet we may say with Stubbs that 'the friars represented the doctrines of civil independence in the Universities and country at large',[100] and we may urge that the author teaches the lesson that the

---

[96] Bémont, *Simon de Montfort*, p. 230.

[97] Ibid, pp. 58, 86   Trivet, *Annales*, s. a. 1276.

[98] Monsieur Bémont refers to this in a note on p. 219, but does not consider its teaching, or the bearing of that teaching on the ideas of de Montfort.

[99] Mr. Kingsford suggests that it is not impossible that the author may have been attached to the earl's household (cf. his edition, p. xviii).

[100] Stubbs, *Const. Hist.* ii 315

community must be governed by a power which is representative and as such limited, and which, because it is thus representative and thus limited, must not act without the advice of the community. Perhaps in Simon's eyes that limit was to be imposed, and that advice given, only by the aristocracy, as the *Forma Regiminis* suggests; perhaps the wider assembly of February 1265 was only intended as an exceptional and as it were 'constituent' assembly to ratify the constitution of 1264.[101] Yet it is a matter of opinion, and some of us may feel that 'community' had for Simon a broader significance, and that the principle of representation, not once, but twice admitted by Simon in the course of 1265, was part of his permanent creed. We may feel that 'community' meant not merely the one particular community of prelates and barons, but a *communa totius terrae*, in which there were federated into one whole the upper community of prelates and barons, and the lower communities of shire and borough; we may feel that such a community, so broad and so deep, can only act through representation, which must always, and not once only, be necessary for its action. And we may suspect that Simon owed such a creed in some measure to the teaching of the friars—the Franciscans, it is true, rather than the Dominicans.[102]

It was left to the two friar-archbishops, Kilwardby the Dominican and Peckham the Franciscan, to make representation a permanent and regular part of the organization of the English Church. Robert Kilwardby, a Dominican who had been provincial prior of his Order in England, held the chair of Canterbury from 1272 to 1278. He had been appointed by Gregory X, in spite of Edward's endeavours on behalf of Burnell, after the three years' vacancy which followed the death of Boniface. Kilwardby was not only an administrator,

---

[101] As M Bémont notes, *op cit*, p 231, the writs of June 1265 do not summon representatives of towns. But he is not quite right in saying that this parliament was to be composed 'only of the higher baronage and the prelates', as we have seen, proctors of chapters are summoned, and the principle of representation is still admitted.

[102] It may be suggested that, if the February parliament of 1265 is treated as 'constituent', it is parallel to the *capitulum generalissimum* in which the Dominicans made constitutional changes. See Addendum II.

but a theologian, and also, as we have seen, a considerable author [103] The accession of Kilwardby, followed as he was by men of the same stamp in Peckham and Winchelsea, inaugurated a new epoch in the history of the English Church. The scene and the actors were both new, and a new drama was played. With the accession of Rudolf of Habsburg in 1273 the conflict of Papacy and Empire was ended, and there came a relaxation of the papal pressure which that had entailed. The relations of the English Church to Rome became less those of hostility and more those of alliance. The character and policy of the new monarch, Edward I, tended in the same direction. Directing his energies to the creation of a united national state, he sought to bring the clergy within its action, *ut esset clerus sicut et populus*,[104] and to compel the clergy to pay their quota to the expenses of the state no longer as a matter of clerical obedience to their papal sovereign, but as a matter of civic duty to the secular government. The English Church, which had fought Henry III because he acted as the colleague or henchman of the Papacy in its demands, had now to resist Edward because he wished to act as independent lay sovereign of the realm.

This was hardly the case in the beginning of the reign. Edward was still the ally of the Papacy, fresh from a Crusade, and the first years of his reign are in ecclesiastical matters not unlike the years of his father's rule The first act of the archbishop elect, in the beginning of the reign of Edward I, was to preside over an episcopal council, which, at the request of two papal nuncios and a bull from Gregory X which they had brought, voted a tenth for two years to Edward and Edmund his brother for the expenses of their Crusade (January 19, 1273).[105] In the next year, at the Second Council of Lyons, Gregory X exacted a tenth from clerical revenues

---

[103] *Supra*, pp. 29–30. Kilwardby must have been a man of considerable character and originality. His theological attitude is independent , and the thorough method he brought to his office of archbishop, and the full use he made of representative institutions, seem to indicate an organiser and a statesman.

[104] *Ann. Osney*, p. 286, quoted in Stubbs, *Select Charters*, p 432.

[105] Wilkins, *Conc.* ii. 24–5, from the Register of Worcester.

for the Crusade for the next six years,[106] 'which was no small grievance and disturbance of all Christianity.' But the new reign soon settled down to a policy of healing. Already in September of 1273 Robert Kilwardby has summoned a representative council, not to grant or resist taxation, but for a purpose for which representation has not hitherto been used—the reform of the Church and the remedy of her troubles. Since the cares of his office have been imposed upon him, he has turned his thoughts to the state of churches and churchmen, and has found much that needs correction and reform with the help of his brothers and co-bishops. And that such business may be supported by sounder counsel, each bishop is to bring three or four of the greater, discreeter, and more prudent persons of his church and diocese,[107] so that by common counsel the business may have a happy issue. The scope and function of representation has here widened. It is used not for taxation merely, but for general deliberation on the business of the Church. Just as there is an advance from the knights of 1254, who answer precisely about an aid, to knights and burgesses of 1275, who treat about the business of the realm,[108] so there is an advance from the clerical assemblies of 1254–8 to this assembly of 1273. The same advance appears in 1277. The issue of some of the reforms attempted of late is uncertain, others are quite unachieved; new difficulties have arisen to the grave peril of the English Church. Once more the Dominican archbishop turns to a representative assembly. Bishops are to come with some greater persons from their chapters, and with archdeacons and proctors of all the clergy of each diocese, to treat of the business aforesaid and by common consent bring it to a laudable end.[109] Here ended the activity of Kilwardby. In 1278 he was made cardinal bishop of Porto, and left England (taking the registers of Canterbury as he went). It was hardly a promotion, and

---

[106] Labbe and Cossart, xi. 1. 995 ; *Ann. Osney*, p. 260.

[107] This seems to embrace representatives both of the cathedral church and of the diocesan clergy. For the summons see Wilkins, *Conc.* ii. 26, and Stubbs, *Select Charters*, p. 455.

[108] *Eng. Hist. Rev.*, 1910, p 236.

[109] Wilkins, *Conc.* ii. 30; Stubbs, *Select Charters*, p. 456.

its real motive, Professor Tout thinks, was 'to remove Kilwardby from England and to send a more active man in his place.'[110] Peckham, his successor, certainly proved himself, as soon as he came, more active; but he failed to check the development of Edward's ecclesiastical policy.

Whatever may have been the papal view of Kilwardby's conduct in his office, he had really brought the Dominican system of government by a representative chapter into the English Church.   He had made a representative provincial synod the regular organ for the conduct of general ecclesiastical business, as the provincial chapter was in his own Order, and no longer an extraordinary method for meeting financial pressure.   In both assemblies too (1273 and 1277) he had included diocesan as well as capitular representatives, and he was the first, if we may except the assemblies from 1256 to 1258, to include representatives of the diocesan clergy in a purely ecclesiastical meeting of the Church   His successor, John Peckham, also a friar, but of the Franciscan Order, who had already been a doctor at Oxford, continued the work he had begun.   At first indeed Peckham took another line. In hot haste he convoked a provincial synod of bishops only at Reading in the middle of 1279, and passed canons against pluralities ('which frightened every benefice hunter among the clerks of the royal household'), and denounced penalties against all violators of Magna Carta ('in a fashion that suggested that the king was an habitual offender').[111]   Later in

---

[110] *Political Hist.* iii. 150 ; cf. also Tout's article in *Dict. Nat Biog* Edward's wife, Eleanor of Castile, was a great friend of the Dominicans. Kilwardby, though appointed against Edward's wishes, may have become a friend of the Court.   But see Addendum III.

[111] Tout, ibid, p. 151.   Was the Statute of Mortmain, passed in November, already mooted'   If so, Peckham may have been trying to raise a storm which would prevent its passing.   His first article of excommunication is against those who presume to deprive the Church of its rights or infringe its liberties.   The excommunication of all violators of Magna Carta in the eleventh, and the provision for posting a copy of 'the charter of the king for the liberty of the Church and realm granted by the king' in cathedral and collegiate churches, may have the same object.   Stubbs speaks of Edward as having 'kept back the statute' (*Const. Hist.* ii. 117).   It would perhaps be too much to suggest that the prospect of such legislation as the Statute of Mortmain explains the going of Kilwardby and the coming of Peckham.

the year, when Mortmain had been passed, and he had been forced to revoke the obnoxious articles, and to order the copies of the Charter to be taken down from the churches,[112] he acted more moderately. On November 15, 1279, Edward I asked for a grant from the clergy. The language of his letter throws light on his policy. He has taken the labours of others on himself to secure the peace of the State · he has spent much on the Welsh expedition, on making castles and towns in Wales, and on gaining an alliance with France. It is just and reasonable that the clergy, who no less than all the rest of the people live under his rule, and enjoy his protection in their things temporal, and specially in their things spiritual, should come to his aid.[113] The demand is of a different order from those which the clergy had had to face in the reign of Henry III there is no speech of a Crusade but of secular objects, there is no papal confirmation, but the king's mere demand, the clergy is not asked as a separate Order, but as part of the realm, enjoying the benefits of its government [114] Peckham bowed to the demand As early as November 6 he summoned a convocation for January 20, 1280 The bishops were to convoke and persuade the clergy of their dioceses, and bring news of the result either in person, or through their proctors, or certainly through proctors proper for the business,[115] to the assembly in January. Similarly, the Archbishop of York ordered each archdeacon in his province to consult his clergy, and bring news of the result to Pomfret with two men of worthy eminence and one dean of the archdeaconry.[116] In the issue Canterbury granted one-fifteenth for three years, and York an equivalent amount of one-tenth for two [117]

But Peckham, though he had raised no opposition in this matter, and though he went out of his way to expedite

---

[112] Wilkins, *Conc* ii 40   [113] Ibid , p 41

[114] Edward's letter seemed worth quoting at some length, because the theory it enunciates is responsible for his attempt, which eventually failed, to incorporate the Church in a united national parliament It is in speaking of Edward's demand in 1279 that the Osney annalist uses the phrase quoted above, *ut esset clerus sicut et populus.*

[115] This seems to leave room for the attendance of proctors of the clergy at the convocation, Wilkins, *Conc* ii 37.

[116] Wilkins, ibid , pp. 41-2.   [117] Ibid., p 42.

a similar demand of the king in 1281,[118] had by no means
entirely submitted.   At the end of July, 1281, he summoned
bishops, abbots, priors, deans, archdeacons, and proctors of
chapters (this is the first certain use of representation made by
him) to a council at Lambeth, in which he sought to vindicate
for the spiritual courts cases of patronage and pleas which
touched the chattels of the spiritualty.[119]. Before the assembly
met, Edward sent the archbishop two letters, prohibiting any
action to the prejudice of the Crown.[120]   The archbishop gave
way : the Constitutions published at Lambeth have nothing
to say of patronage or pleas touching personalty.   Though
the question of clerical jurisdiction was raised again by Peckham
in 1285, when the clergy of Canterbury petitioned for the regulation of royal prohibitions, the only result which he achieved
by his persistence was a further limitation of the province of
spiritual courts.[121]

Between 1281 and 1285 two important developments appeared in the history of Convocation, the one in 1282, the
other in 1283   They are the last two that we have to trace.
In 1281 the influence of clerical organization on secular is seen
in a curious way.   Corresponding to the two provinces and
two provincial synods of Canterbury and York, the North
and the South, Edward I in 1282 summoned two assemblies,
the one for the North at York, the other for the South at
Northampton.   Both assemblies met in two bodies, the one
lay, the other clerical.   The lay body in either assembly
consisted of magnates and elected knights and burgesses ; the
clerical body of bishops, abbots, priors, and other heads of
religious houses, with proctors on behalf of the dean and

---

[118] Wilkins, *Conc.* ii. 49–50.

[119] *Ann Osney*, p. 285 (quoted in *Select Charters*, p. 432)

[120] Wilkins, ii 50   This suggests the *constitutio* of William I, quoted by
Eadmer (*Select Charters*, p 82)

[121] Professor Tout goes too far in saying that in 1281 'once more
Edward annulled the proceedings of a council ' (*Political Hist.* iii. 152)
Strictly speaking, even in 1279 the proceedings were revoked by the
archbishop (Wilkins, ii. 40) and not annulled by the king ; and on this
occasion, as the proceedings had never taken place, they could not be
annulled.   The general reference of the writ *circumspecte agatis* to 1285
is perhaps wrong ; cf. Pollock and Maitland, *H. E. L.*, ii. 200.   The date
of the writ is dubious : Prynne referred it to *c.* 1316.

chapter of each diocese.[122]   Here we have the first instance of a royal summons to clerical representatives since 1265, but the summons, as in 1265, is confined to proctors of chapters. This limitation explains the issue of the assembly, as far as the clergy were concerned.   Asked for one-tenth of their revenues for three years, the clergy at Northampton replied that they could not act in the absence of the larger portion of their numbers; and it was ordered that all the clergy of the province of Canterbury should be summoned to give an answer.   Peckham accordingly on January 21, 1283, alleging in the preamble of his summons this order (and not, apparently, acting on his own initiative), summoned to a clerical assembly, to be held in London at Easter, bishops, abbots, priors, heads of religious houses, deans and archdeacons.   He further enjoined the bishops each to assemble the clergy of his diocese, and expound the king's demands, so that from each diocese two proctors in the name of the clergy, and from each chapter one, should be sent with sufficient instructions and full and express power of treating and consenting.[123]   The convocation met at Easter; but a new meeting, in the same form, had to be summoned for Michaelmas to give the diocesan synods more time, and it was not until November that a grant was finally made to the king.

Here we have the final form of Convocation, in which it afterwards persisted, with the two proctors from each diocese, and one from each chapter.   It cannot be said that Peckham himself was to any extent responsible for its determination. He had indeed summoned proctors of chapters to Lambeth himself in 1281; but the summons of 1282 proceeded from the king, and the extension of that summons in 1283 to include proctors of the diocesan clergy was due to the action of the clergy assembled at Northampton under the royal summons.

[122] Wilkins, ii. 91 ; Stubbs, *Select Charters*, p 466   Wilkins thought that the two bodies of the York assembly were treated as one, and summoned by one writ (not, as in the Southern province, by two separate writs). Certainly the king directs a single writ announcing that he has appointed Antony Bek and the Archbishop of York to act on his behalf, to bishops, abbots, priors, chapters, and their proctors, knights, freemen, communities, and all others, as if they were one body (Wilkins, ii. 93)

[23] Wilkins, ii. 93–5 , Stubbs, *Select Charters*, pp. 466–7.

It is on the anvil of taxation that Convocation was finally beaten into shape.   The form of 1283 was afterwards treated as authoritative, and was regarded as a canon, though it was no canon.[124]   It applied to the province of Canterbury : the convocation of York, as in the assembly at Pomfret in 1280, continued to have two proctors from each archdeaconry.[125] The stamp of royal confirmation served to make the form of 1283 authoritative.   In summoning the clergy to Parliament in 1294, Edward introduces the clause which, except for one or two verbal alterations made in 1295,[126] is henceforth regular Each bishop must attend, 'premonishing (in 1294 'summoning') the dean and chapter of his cathedral church and the archdeacons and all the clergy of his diocese—causing the dean and archdeacons to attend in their proper persons and the chapter through one, the clergy through two fit proctors with full and sufficient power' The form the Church had adopted for its own provincial synod is used by the king for the inclusion of the Church as one of the estates of the realm in parliament.

Here the development, in Aristotle's phrase, has attained its end.   We ought indeed to note that Edward's plan of including the Church in parliament as one of the elements of a united national state failed.   Within the next forty years it had been practically decided that the Church, as such, should have no lot or part in parliament.   Thus what had been attempted probably in 1254, certainly in 1255, again in 1265, in 1282, in 1294, and in 1295—the inclusion of the clergy in general through their representatives in a national parliament—ceases after the reign of Edward I to be attempted in fact, though it is done in legal theory to this very day.   There remains only the provincial synod (or rather the synods of York and Canterbury) for the clergy sitting by themselves.   This, however, has two different aspects.   There are sessions of the synod summoned by the archbishop *proprio motu* for purely ecclesiastical business, 'the extirpation of heresy, the reform

.   [124] Stubbs, *Const. Hist* ii 207   [125] *Supra*, n. 116.
[126] The forms of summons in 1294 and 1295 are practically identical. The important difference is that Edward in 1294 summoned the clergy for a different date than that fixed for the laity, he treated it as separate.   In and after 1295 the clergy and laity are summoned for the same time.

of manners, the dealings with foreign Churches and general councils.' [127] There are sessions held in consequence of a request or a command issued by the king with a view to a grant of money, when the synod meets at about the same time as parliament, and should, if the *praemunientes* clause were followed, meet at the same place, and not as a separate synod, but as a section of parliament. Proceedings in sessions of the former kind were independent of the king; but he might nevertheless, as in 1281, oppose a practical veto. On the other hand, proceedings in sessions of the latter kind were not confined to the voting of taxes, and might be devoted in part to ecclesiastical matters. We must not conceive the synod, even in its quasi-parliamentary aspect as a tax-voting body, as an adjunct or part of parliament. It is not summoned by the king through writs addressed to the bishops: it is summoned by the archbishop, at the king's request, through letters issued to the bishops. In other words, it is still a provincial synod, an assembly of the Church as such, and no part of a secular parliament [128]

Of the diocesan councils of the thirteenth century little need here be said. They contained the whole clergy of the diocese (*totus clerus dioeceseos*) [129] meeting as a primary assembly or *presbyterium*. In them were issued the constitutions of the bishop; and as the pressure of taxation grew

---

[127] Stubbs, *Const. Hist.* iii. 331.

[128] If we apply these distinctions to the period which we have considered (practically 1226-95) we find four varieties: (1) the provincial synod proper, which may be convoked to meet a papal demand, as in 1226, or, more according to its essence, to regulate the state of the Church, as in 1273 and 1277, or in 1279 (at Reading) and 1281 (at Lambeth), (2) the provincial synod which meets to answer a royal demand for taxes, and which is like the later convocation when engaged in voting a clerical tenth (cf. the second meeting of 1226, the meeting of 1280, and the meetings of 1283); (3) the meeting which is partly a provincial synod, partly a part of parliament—the former, since it meets either as a separate body from the lay assembly, as in 1282, or at a separate time, as in 1294; the latter, since it is convoked by royal writ (under this head may also be placed the meetings of the clergy in 1254 (if a meeting took place then) and in 1255); (4) the meeting of the same elements as those which compose a provincial synod, but as part of parliament, and not as a provincial synod (e g. in 1295). We may add legatine councils of the whole Church, under the presidency of a papal *legatus a latere* (as in 1237); cf Stubbs, *Const. Hist* ii. 208.

[129] Wilkins, ii. 25 (the Synod of the diocese of Norwich at Eyam).

they, like the shire-court, were consulted about its imposition
and incidence. In 1254, when proctors begin to appear on
behalf of the clergy of the diocese (or as in 1255 of the archdeaconry), the diocesan clergy were possibly thus consulted,
and after consultation appointed their representatives.[130] In
1283 Peckham definitely instructs the bishops to assemble the
clergy of their diocese, and expound the king's demands, that
proctors with full instructions may be sent.[131] At York in
1280 the archdeacons are directed to convoke their clergy
and expound the king's demands, so that, with representatives
of their archdeaconry, they may come to give an answer on
behalf of the community of all the archdeaconry.[132] We shall
probably not be wrong in concluding that the diocesan synod
awoke in this way to a more vigorous life under the pressure
of taxation, and that its meetings became far more frequent.[133]

On the whole we may say that this English development is
unique. Whatever the constitutional development of the
Spanish Cortes, the provincial synods of Spain attain no
more than representation of chapters. In Germany one can
hardly discover that even the representation of chapters is
regular in provincial synods, though in diocesan synods,
which ought to be attended by all the clergy of the diocese,
representatives of chapters and collegiate churches and even
of the diocesan clergy appear. The development of France
approaches nearest to that of England; but France differs
from England. The French provincial synod by the fourteenth
century includes representatives of chapters; it does not
include representatives of the diocesan clergy. The États

---

[130] *Supra*, pp 55-6   [131] *Supra*, p. 67.
[132] I take it that the reply would be given in a provincial synod of the
whole of the province of York   Stubbs (*Const Hist.* ii 205) speaks
of the diocesan synods of the province giving their 'several consent'.
But, two pages further on (ibid., p. 207), he speaks of the convocation of
the province of York in this connexion, and though it is true Wilkins
prints only the response of the clergy of the *diocese* of York (ii. 42), I take
it that the clergy of the other dioceses also responded in the same sense
in a general synod along with the clergy of York.
[133] Cf *supra*, note 19   Hauck, *op. cit*, v 1 180, remarks that generally
speaking the diocesan synod is not a legislative body like the provincial
synod: the bishop enacts constitutions in it, but not by its consent, and
its powers of consent to diocesan taxation are very slight. This would
hardly be true of England at the end of the thirteenth century.

Généraux include representatives of convents and chapters, because convents and chapters stand on the feudal ladder; they do not include representatives of the diocesan clergy. The proctors of the chapters continue to sit in the États Généraux. the representatives of our clergy withdraw from Parliament. To what shall we ascribe this difference of development ? Why does the English synod assume a more democratic form ? And why has it a more regular composition (for that of the continental synod seems variable) and greater frequency of action ? One naturally turns in the first place to geography. The distance of England from Rome permits England to develop on its own line. the primacy of Canterbury makes the developments which take place in the province of Canterbury authoritative for the whole country. Other countries stood closer to Rome: other countries were divided into a number of equal and independent provinces. Canterbury was, if we may use the word, more 'national' than Reims or Mainz or Toledo.[134] In the second place, differences of historical development were active. The papal pressure, which helped to bring about the representation of the chapters and inferior clergy, was indeed felt elsewhere than in England. though England, temporally as well as spiritually subject to papal supremacy, perhaps felt that pressure more than other countries. The financial pressure of the lay state, more highly organized in England, especially on its financial side, than in other countries, perhaps constituted a greater differentia On the other hand, we must admit that the French monarchy, from the time of the Second Crusade, imposed tenths on clerical goods, sometimes with and sometimes without papal authorization.[135] We are thus driven to find a differentia less in the imposition of taxation, than in the attitude of the country towards such imposition. Now the English attitude in the thirteenth century is already something like 'No taxation without representation': the French attitude was not. Already

---

[134] I do not mean to assert that the English Church had any peculiar independence of Rome in e g. legislation

[135] Cf Viollet, *op cit*, ii. 402–6, iii 477–80 It is noteworthy that the Avignonese captivity made it easy for the kings to get papal authorization, without troubling about further consent.

in Magna Carta we find that extraordinary aids and scutages need the consent of *Magnum Concilium*; already in 1226 we find the chapters voting their sixteenth by representatives; already in 1240 we find Matthew Paris representing the bishops as quoting the principle that what touches all must be approved by all. Strong in the strength of this principle, the clergy claim and gain representation. The first taxation for the benefit of the Crown (apart from the ransom of Richard I, which is exceptional) fell on clerical revenues in 1226, the same year saw the chapters represented in the assembly that granted the tax. The first taxation to which the shires are asked to give their consent through representative knights falls in 1254; probably in that same year, and certainly in 1255, representatives of the diocesan clergy also appear. The representation of the vigorous local life of the shire (after all the supreme differentia of England from the rest of Western Europe) finds its counterpart in, and lends its support to, the representation of the clergy of archdeaconries and dioceses, who are bound up in that local life—for has not the priest gone along with the reeve and representatives of the vill from early days?[136] Similarly, the representative parliament finds its counterpart in the representative convocation; either supports and stiffens the other, and a parliament broad in its composition, permanent in its membership, regular in its sessions, postulates a convocation as broad, as permanent, as regular. Thus we should find in the strength of a representative principle permeating both clergy and laity, in the strength of a local life in which the clergy share with the laity, in the strength of a national representative system expressing that principle and drawing vigour from that local life, the reasons for the nature of the English convocation

But does this involve the consequence that clerical representation is drawn from and modelled upon secular representation? Hardly. We would rather urge that the clergy are the forerunners, and that through their habits of organized

---

[136] Stubbs, *Select Charters*, p. 86 (priest, reeve, and six villeins of each vill on the Domesday juries); p. 105 (reeve, priest, and four better men of the vill attending shire-court).

action and their legal ideas of procuration they lead the movement to representation There are two main ideas underlying the English representative system of the thirteenth century—indeed from the thirteenth to the nineteenth century. In the first place the representation is representation of communities. It is representation not of geographical constituencies containing some thousands of electoral units, but of organized and organic communities, that have a real and regular life of their own. The House of Commons is a federation of these communities through their representatives : it expresses the mediaeval conception of the State as a *communitas communitatum*. In the second place the representative is a full representative He binds his constituents. He is a proxy with full powers of attorney, there is no room for a referendum to his constituents. The knights and burgesses, says Edward in 1295, shall have full and sufficient powers for themselves *and their communities*, and business shall in no wise remain undone for want of such power.[137] Both of these ideas are at home with the clergy. Their chapters are real communities, which can federate in a joint assembly, and are conscious of the reasons and the need of such federation, as early as 1226. With the nature of a *procuratorium* they are well acquainted ; their chapters and monasteries have to send proctors to Rome as a matter of ordinary legal business, and Rome will invite proctors, from chapters at any rate, to a general Council of the Church. The reinforcement of the baronage by shire and borough representatives, which makes a national parliament, finds its precedent in the reinforcement of the episcopate by the proctors of chapters Representation in a clerical parliament in 1226 is nearly thirty years prior to representation in the lay assembly of 1254. We may repeat the saying of Viollet : ' Je suppose que ces réunions ecclésiastiques ont pu contribuer à faciliter le développement et la régularisation des grandes assemblées civiles, des réunions d'états. . . . En effet, le premier des trois états, le clergé, se trouva, du premier jour, habitué et comme rompu à ce que nous appellerions aujourd'hui les usages parlementaires.

[137] Stubbs, *Select Charters*, p. 486.

Circonstance heureuse qui a dû contribuer, dans l'Europe entière, sinon à former, du moins à regularisci la tenue des états.'[138]   Stubbs has remarked that the mediaeval procedure of parliament is like that of convocation.   There is the same list of *gravamina*, the same petition for remedy.[139]   And so we may urge that the Church by its organization, its ideas, its procedure, was a model and a precedent for that parliamentary system, which, we must admit and indeed urge, in turn reacted on the Church; for the regular parliamentary system of Convocation would have been impossible, unless it had found a parallel and a support in a national parliament, and unless it had been part of a whole structure of society which was consonant with itself.

And what of the Dominicans ?   Well, they are a part of that development of representation in the General Councils of the Church, in the provincial synod, and even (in Germany) in the diocesan synod, which marks the thirteenth century. In that development they appear early, as early as 1221, of that development they are the highest expression, for the use of representation was regular and systematic through the whole Order.   They are a new Order, and they have the attraction of novelty; they are an Order with a high prestige, and their prestige will make them a model.   They found friends for themselves in great men, like Stephen Langton and Simon de Montfort; and great men can give a vogue to ideas and practices which would otherwise pass unregarded, making a commonplace original, and a fantasy a practical policy. They had communicated their organization to an Order which

---

[138] Viollet, *op cit*, ii 355

[139] *Const Hist* iii 1479   'It is not improbable that this process was identical with that by which in the discussions of the ecclesiastical convocations the *gravamina* of individuals, the *reformanda* or proposed remedies, and the *articuli cleri* or completed representations sent up to the house of bishops are and have been from the very first framed and treated   The *gravamina* of individual members of convocation answer to the initiatory act of the individual member in the commons, and the *articuli cleri* to the *communes petitiones*.'   One may even suggest that the two Houses of Convocation may have been something of a precedent for the two Houses of Parliament, and have helped to produce that accidental bicameral system which, consecrated by time, has been defended as a theoretical ideal and imitated as a political model

had a greater attraction, and certainly a far greater vogue, than their own : the Franciscans after 1239 reproduced many of the features of the statesmanship of St. Dominic.[140] These are all so many channels of indirect influence. Direct influence can hardly be proved. That Stephen Langton had felt their influence when he admitted representation as far as he did in 1226 is only conjecture. That de Montfort, who from early years had been connected with the Order, felt and expressed their influence is equally conjectural, if perhaps a little more possible That Kilwardby, himself a Dominican and ex-prior of the English province, was translating their ideas into practice in 1273 and 1277 is, at the least, very probable. But we may content ourselves with asserting as a certainty, that they are the highest expression of the development of the representative principle in the thirteenth-century Church, and that the indirect influence of that expression must have been felt in the Church and to some extent in the State.

One lesson which emerges from this study may be remarked in conclusion. The study of the institutional development of the Middle Ages is an organic whole. We cannot isolate Church and State , not only do they develop side by side, but they interact in their development. The development of representation in Church and State must not be figured in the mind as the advance of two parallel lines in two separate squares ; it is the growth of one idea into an institution, in that one and single *respublica Christiana* under two governments (the *regnum* and the *sacerdotium*) of which Dr. Figgis

[140] This, of course, did not prevent a good deal of friction between the two Orders. There is an interesting passage of arms, illustrating this rivalry, in Wilkins, *Conc* ii 109–10 A Dominican at Oxford has crossed without leave to the Franciscan Order at Oxford, and the prior and friars of the Dominican house have excommunicated the Franciscans. It is a canonical rule that a regular may go from a lower to a higher Order (as for instance to-day one may leave any Order for the Carthusian) ; and Peckham, assuming that his own Order is higher than the Dominican, at once is up in arms Another interesting, if fussy, letter is directed against the provincial prior of the Dominicans, who had said that Peckham's friends did not incite him to the martyrdom of St. Thomas (p. 111), and divulged a private conversation ! This letter reminds one of Trivet's description of Peckham (*Annales*, s. a 1279) as *ordinis zelator praecipuus, gestus affatusque pompatici*. On the whole matter cf A. G. Little, *Grey Friars in Oxford*, pp. 73 sqq.

has taught us to conceive.[141]   Further, we must not in our insular way isolate the institutional development of England from that of continental Europe.   We have learned of late not to contrast English with continental feudalism, but to see in both the same plant growing under somewhat different conditions   We have been taught by recent historians to think of the municipal development of the Middle Ages in Western Europe as a single whole, and of its problems as not to be solved country by country, but rather to be treated on the same lines for all countries taken together.[142]   The development of representation must be treated in the same way, it is a general movement in all Western Europe in the thirteenth century, and it must be regarded as such if it is to be understood in its fullness.

[141] *Trans Roy Hist Soc*, 1911, vol v, pp 63 sqq. Cf. also Dr. Troeltsch, *Die Soziallehre der christlichen Kirchen*, cap II, esp p 182

[142] Cf. M Pirenne, *Revue Historique*, liii 82 : 'De même qu'on ne distingue pas une féodalité française et une féodalité allemande, de m me aussi il n'y a pas lieu d'établir une ligne de démarcation entre les villes allemandes et les villes françaises.'   As M. Pirenne refuses to distinguish France from Germany, so the English historian must refuse to distinguish England from either

ADDENDA

I. p. 30   The vogue of the Dominicans in England during the
thirteenth century may be still further illustrated   Father Jarrett has
drawn my attention to the fact that Hubert de Burgh, the justiciar
of Henry III, left land in Ireland and his London house to the
Order, and was buried in one of its chapels (Matt. Paris, iv. 243).
John of Darlington, one of the most striking figures in the early
history of the Order, became confessor and councillor to Henry III
in 1256 ; was one of the Committee of Twenty-four in 1258 , and
was employed in political negotiations as well as in ecclesiastical
business afterwards   A considerable scholar, and joint author with
Richard of Stavensby and Hugh of Croydon of the English Concordances (Quétif and Echard, *Scriptores Ord Praed.* i. 209), he
was Archbishop of Dublin when he died in 1284 (see Trivet, *Annales,*
s a 1276, 1279, 1284)   The fact that Dominican friars were as much
the favourites of men like Stephen Langton and Hubert de Burgh
as of Henry III seems to show that they did not belong to one side
in politics (*supra,* p 58, n. 92), but had friends equally in both camps
With the English episcopate they were in especially close connexion
Edmund Rich, Archbishop of Canterbury, had continually members
of the Order in his company, and had been the companion of the
Dominican Robert Bacon in the schools (Trivet, s a 1240) , Richard,
Bishop of Chichester, had a Dominican confessor (*ibid,* s a 1252)
These instances belong to the reign of Henry III , but the Dominicans
did not cease to flourish under Edward I   A story in Trivet's *Annals*
(s a 1281) shows Hugh of Manchester, provincial prior of the Order,
in intimate contact with the king ; and in 1294 Hugh was sent by
Edward I on a political mission to France along with a Franciscan
friar.   In 1286 Trivet records the presence both of Edward I and of
Philip IV at a meeting of the general chapter of the Order at Paris
   The main authority for the Dominicans in England in the thirteenth
century is Trivet, himself a Dominican   Details of the lives and
writings of particular friars are given in Quétif and Echard's *Scriptores*
(see especially under the year 1228, on John of St. Giles , 1248, on

Bacon and Fishacre ; 1248, on Mauclerk ; 1279, on Kilwardby ; 1284, on John of Darlington , 1290, on Claypole ; and 1298, on William of Hutton, Archbishop of Dublin)

II. p. 61 It is a question deserving of consideration, how far clerical machinery was ever adopted and utilized for political and secular purposes during the Middle Ages The constitutional novelties which occur in the years 1258–65 seem certainly to be based in some cases on ecclesiastical precedents, such as would readily offer themselves to de Montfort and his clerical colleagues. The employment, for instance, of electors to elect an executive committee, which we find both in the Provisions of Oxford and in the *Forma Regiminis*, seems to me a direct imitation of the plan adopted by the Dominican Order (and on its analogy by the Franciscan ; see *supra*, p 23, n 38) of electing *definitores per disquisitionem* of three nominators In fact de Montfort in the *Forma Regiminis* employs just the same number of nominators (cf. Stubbs, *Select Charters*, p 413, with *Constit Fr Praed* , Paris, 1886, pp 419–20). I would almost venture to suggest that the use of the committees themselves, which is so marked a feature of the years 1258–65, is the result of imitation of the ecclesiastical institution of *definitores.*

III p 64 Père Mandonnet suggests to me that Kilwardby, who was not a Thomist, was recalled owing to the representations made at Rome by the Thomist party. Certainly the division between the Thomists and the other body of opinion to which Kilwardby belonged (see *supra*, p 30) led to controversy in the Order On this hypothesis the Pope's motive in recalling Kilwardby would be theological, and not, as Professor Tout suggests, political

INDEX

OXFORD: HORACE HART M A.
PRINTER TO THE UNIVERSITY